LAS VEGAS

Glitter to Gourmet

LAS VEGAS

Glitter to Gourmet

Savory and Sensational Recipes
from the Junior League of *Las Vegas*

Las Vegas
Glitter to Gourmet

Published by the Junior League of Las Vegas
© Copyright 2001 by the Junior League of Las Vegas
http://www.jllv.org

Library of Congress Number: 00-134319
ISBN: 0-9614100-4-3

Edited, designed, and manufactured by
Favorite Recipes® Press,
an imprint of

FRP

2451 Atrium Way
Nashville, Tennessee 37214
1-800-358-0560

Designer: Steve Newman
Managing Editor: Mary Cummings
Project Editor: Judy Jackson

Manufactured in the United States of America
First Printing: 2001   20,000 copies

Pictured on front cover: Shrimp Cocktail "Martini Style"
(recipe on page 19)

Introduction

Today, visitors strolling the Las Vegas Strip can witness pirate ships battling on the high seas, a volcano erupting, roller coasters wrapping hotels, gondolas gliding along canals, waters dancing, and the *glitter* of the famous dazzling neon signs. Visitors can experience imaginary realms and far-away places such as Mandalay, Paris, Ancient Egypt, and Rome, the world of Aladdin, Medieval England, and the Orient. Re-creations of locales known for celebration and gourmet cuisine, such as Rio, New York, and New Orleans, tempt those looking for excitement. Add to this Downtown Las Vegas, which boasts the largest *glittering* light and sound show in the world, the four-block-long Fremont Street Experience . . . there is no place like Las Vegas!

In this city known for its action-packed casinos and glitzy nightlife, a new ambiance has emerged. Las Vegas has become a mecca for renowned restaurants and chefs with the most impressive of credentials—all intent on satisfying the most international and discriminating *gourmet* palates. Our cookbook, *Glitter to Gourmet*, is not only a reflection of the pulse of our city and the talents of our resident chefs, it is a portrait of those who live in our community: gracious hosts and hostesses who share their treasured family recipes and hints for entertaining at home . . . a formal dinner . . . alfresco fare on the patio . . . a champagne brunch. This is the *Glitter to Gourmet* of Las Vegas.

The Junior League of Las Vegas

The Junior League of Las Vegas is an organization of women committed to promoting voluntarism, developing the potential of women, and improving the community through effective action and leadership of trained volunteers. Its purpose is exclusively educational and charitable.

—Mission Statement

In 1996, the Junior League of Las Vegas celebrated its 50th year of being a visible force and voice for positive change in our ever-growing community. We continue to develop and institute projects that become known community institutions for Las Vegas and Nevada. In the past five decades, our projects and programs have addressed specific needs in our community. Hundreds of health, medical, cultural, social, and educational programs and services have benefited from Junior League support. Past and present projects include:

Ronald McDonald House of Greater Las Vegas
Shade Tree Shelter for Women and Children
Two fire safety houses: Clark County and Las Vegas Fire Departments
Lied Children's Discovery Museum
DARE
HELP of Southern Nevada
Community Alternative Sentencing Program (CAS)
Repeat Boutique Thrift Shop
Ritzy Rummage Sale
Sustainer Holiday Bear Project
Read Aloud Nevada!
Done in a Day community service projects
Education grants to southern Nevada teachers
Community grants to southern Nevada programs
Whitehead House and Beckley House historical restoration and relocation
Jingle Bell Jog
Child Watch

As we enter the new century, the Junior League remains committed to being a positive force and voice for positive change in our community. By training volunteers, providing community programs, and developing the potential of women, we are dedicated to making Las Vegas a better place for all. Our approach to community service is to identify a need, develop a project to meet that need, ensure the success of the project, and, at the appropriate time, turn it over to the community. This process has served both Las Vegas and the Junior League of Las Vegas well. We intend to continue it into the twenty-first century, making a difference in the future as we have in the past.

Glitter to Gourmet Committee

Cookbook Chairmen

2000–2001 Kellie Creekmore-Guild
1999–2000 LuAnn Kutch and Heather Choueiri-Orfaly
1998–1999 Shirley Fentz
1997–1998 Jacklyn Rhinehart
1996–1997 Betsy Horne

Sustaining Advisors

Ann Evans
Nancy Gasho
Marti Hafen
Debbie Levy
Priscilla Scalley

Committee Members

Erin Bendavid
Rochelle Bernstein
Lori Burns
Heather Choueiri-Orfaly
Diana Corazzi
Kellie Creekmore-Guild
Karen Denys
Pat Downs
Shirley Fentz
Tara Fink
Katherine Krucker
Elizabeth Manning
Cristen McCormick

Shenandoah Merrick
Gretchen Papez
Jacklyn Rhinehart
Denise Rose
Sally Rycroft
Mollie Schneider
Dana Sheehan
Terry Sindelar
Shaynee Smith
Caroline Sobota
Ann Trobough
Julie Wolf
Paula Zona

Special thanks to Carol Kehl, Junior League Office Manager

We dedicate this book to those who have made and those who continue to make our city a warm and desirable place to live.

Contents

Opening Acts
Appetizers, Soups and Salads

Champagne Brunch
Breads and Brunch

Lounge Acts
Vegetables and Side Dishes

Patrons

Sous Chefs

Cashman family
Ruth's Chris Steakhouse
Southern Wine and Spirits of Nevada
Southwest Cancer Clinic

Silver Spoons

Janice Allen
Hope Anstett
Patricia Baldwin
Judy Beal
Erin Bendavid
Michelle Betancort
Amy Blanchard
Lucia Bridenstine
Patricia Brinton
Mary Cashman
Heather Choueiri-Orfaly
Deni Conrad
Diana Corazzi
Katherine Dalvey-Bonar
Karen Diamond
Lovee duBoef Arum
Shirley Fentz
Jane Fielden
Nancy Gasho
Joanne Goldberg
Jeanne Greenawalt
Dinah Groce
Kris Hadzicki
Cristen Hansen

Linda Hargrave
Barbara Henry
Lynne Hunter
Julie Keen
Helen Klatt
Diane Kneeland
Sydney Knott
Tracey Krause
Katherine Krucker
Susan Kubat
LuAnn Kutch
Nancy Leslie
Mary Lott
Dr. Kathleen Mahon
Melinda Margolis
Robbie McClain
Denise O. McGuinn
Mary Jo Miller
Dedee Nave
Denise Olsen
Joe and Gretchen Papez
Irene Perer
Lynn Plummer
Cynthia Pridgen

Maria Quirk
Jacklyn Rhinehart
Betsy Rhodes
Elizabeth Roper
Denise Rose
Joyce Rose-Thompson
Carol Rumbolz
Sally Rycroft
Priscilla Scalley
Sandy Seiler-Klopp
Mary Lou Sennes
Michele Shafe
Dana Sheehan
Robin Singleton
Carolyn M. Sparks
Carole Terry
LaVerne Thompson
Sandra Tiberti
Troy and Ann Trobough
Lynn Wiesner
Lynda Wohletz
Karen Zamboni
Lois Zellers

Acknowledgments

The Junior League of Las Vegas sincerely appreciates

Ogara Bissell, Photography
Susan Massey, Food Stylist
Las Vegas Convention and Visitor Authority
Las Vegas Chamber of Commerce
Southern Wine and Spirits of Nevada

for their assistance in the development of
Las Vegas Glitter to Gourmet

And the following chefs and celebrities for
the recipes they so graciously contributed

Susan Anton
Bill Bayno
Senator Richard Bryan
Lance Burton
David Cassidy
Chef Sheila Conway
Chef Terry Fong
Chef Henry Garcia
Mayor Oscar Goodman
Chef Stanton Ho
Chef Chris Johns
Stephanie Markham
Phyllis McGuire
Rosie O'Donnell
Chef Jean-Louis Palladin
Chef James Perillo
Chef William Pfersching
Chef Wolfgang Puck
Senator Harry Reid
Chef Michael Ty
Chef James Wierzelenski
Chef Steve Zucker

Opening Acts

Appetizers, Soups and Salads

pictured at left: Red and Green Holiday Salad
(recipe on page 52)

Broiled Olive Hors d'Oeuvre

1 cup coarsely chopped black olives
1/2 cup chopped pimento-stuffed olives
1 1/2 cups shredded sharp Cheddar cheese
1/2 cup mayonnaise
1 to 2 garlic cloves, minced
2 tablespoons finely chopped red onion, or
    1 bunch green onions, finely chopped
1/2 teaspoon curry powder
6 sourdough English muffins, split, or sliced French bread

Combine the black olives, stuffed olives, cheese, mayonnaise, garlic, onion
and curry powder in a bowl and mix well. Spread the mixture on the muffin
halves. Place on a baking sheet and broil until bubbly. Remove to a cutting
surface and cut into quarters. Serve hot.

Yield: 4 dozen

Italian Olive Bread

3 ounces cream cheese, softened
3 tablespoons butter, softened
1 tablespoon mayonnaise
2 small garlic cloves, minced
1/4 teaspoon salt
1/8 teaspoon dried oregano
1/2 cup grated Parmesan cheese
1 loaf Italian bread, split lengthwise
Paprika to taste
1/2 cup sliced pimento-stuffed green olives
1/2 cup sliced black olives

Mix the cream cheese, butter, mayonnaise, garlic, salt and oregano in a
bowl. Stir in the Parmesan cheese. Spread on the cut surfaces of the
bread. Sprinkle with paprika; top with the sliced olives. Reassemble
the loaf and wrap in foil. Place on a baking sheet. Bake at 400 degrees
for 20 minutes. Remove the foil. Slice the bread and serve warm.

Yield: 8 to 12 servings

Bruschetta

1 cup extra-virgin olive oil
4 to 6 garlic cloves, minced
24 (1/2-inch) baguette slices
4 large tomatoes, chopped
1 cup coarsely chopped fresh basil
12 ounces mozzarella cheese, shredded
2 tablespoons extra-virgin olive oil
1 tablespoon red wine vinegar
1 to 2 garlic cloves, minced
Salt and pepper to taste

For the toast, mix 1 cup olive oil and 4 to 6 garlic cloves in a bowl. Let stand for 30 minutes. Brush both sides of the baguette slices generously with the mixture. Place on a baking sheet. Bake at 350 degrees for 20 minutes or until golden brown and crisp. Remove to a serving plate.

For the topping, mix the tomatoes, basil, cheese, 2 tablespoons olive oil, vinegar and 1 to 2 garlic cloves in a bowl. Season with salt and pepper. Let stand for 30 minutes or longer. Spoon the topping onto the toasted baguette slices and serve immediately.

NOTE: Let guests spread the topping themselves to prevent soggy toast.

Yield: 2 dozen

Most Romantic City in the World

There are approximately fifty wedding chapels in Las Vegas.

In 1998, there were 110,164 wedding licenses issued in Las Vegas.

During Valentine's Day weekend in 1999, a total of 2,735 wedding licenses were issued.

The Las Vegas metropolitan area boasts an average of 9,180 weddings a month, or 301 weddings a day.

Historically, the most popular wedding day in Las Vegas is Valentine's Day, with New Year's Eve being the second most popular.

Roquefort Brandy Baguette

1/2 cup crumbled Roquefort cheese
1/3 cup chopped green onions
2 tablespoons butter, softened
2 tablespoons brandy
1 tablespoon mayonnaise
24 (1/4-inch) baguette slices, lightly buttered

Combine the Roquefort cheese, green onions, butter, brandy and mayonnaise in a bowl and mix well. Spread the cheese mixture thinly on the buttered baguette slices. Place on a baking sheet and broil until the cheese is slightly browned. Serve immediately.

Yield: 2 dozen

Shrimp Toast Canapés

8 ounces cooked shrimp, peeled, deveined, chopped
3/4 cup shredded Cheddar cheese
3/4 cup mayonnaise
1/4 cup chopped onion
1 teaspoon Worcestershire sauce
1/2 teaspoon dry mustard
1/4 teaspoon curry powder
Sliced French bread or cocktail rye bread

Combine the shrimp, cheese, mayonnaise, onion, Worcestershire sauce, dry mustard and curry powder in a bowl and mix well. Spread on the bread slices. Place on a baking sheet and broil for 5 minutes or until bubbly. Serve immediately.

VARIATION: Broil on English muffins instead of French bread and serve as open-face sandwiches.

Yield: about 2 dozen

Cheesy Pesto Pizza

1 large prepared pizza crust
3/4 to 1 cup pesto sauce
2 garlic cloves, minced
1 cup shredded mozzarella cheese
1/2 cup grated Parmesan cheese

Place the pizza crust on a baking sheet. Spread the pesto sauce over the crust. Sprinkle with the garlic and top with the mozzarella cheese and Parmesan cheese. Bake at 450 degrees for 9 to 10 minutes or until the cheese bubbles. Place on a cutting board and blot the surface with a paper towel to remove any excess liquid. Let cool for several minutes. Cut into wedges or small squares to serve.

Yield: 8 servings

Brie Crisps

4 ounces ripe Brie cheese, softened
1/2 cup (1 stick) butter, softened
2/3 cup flour
1/4 to 3/8 teaspoon ground red pepper, or to taste
1/8 teaspoon salt
Paprika to taste

Combine the cheese and butter in a food processor container and process until smooth. Add the flour, red pepper and salt and process until a ball begins to form. Turn the dough onto a large piece of plastic wrap. Shape the dough loosely into a 2-inch-diameter cylinder. Wrap in the plastic wrap and chill for 30 minutes. Remove the plastic wrap and shape the dough into a smooth and even cylinder 1 1/2 inches in diameter and 8 inches long. Wrap the roll in plastic wrap and chill overnight.

Slice the roll into 1/4-inch rounds and place 2 inches apart on an ungreased baking sheet. Bake at 400 degrees for 10 to 12 minutes or until the edges are golden brown. Sprinkle with paprika. Serve hot.

Yield: 3 dozen

Red Pepper Jelly

24 red bell peppers, seeded
2 tablespoons salt
4 cups vinegar
6 cups sugar

Purée the bell peppers in batches in a food processor. Transfer the puréed peppers to a large saucepan. Sprinkle the salt over the peppers and let stand for 3 hours. Press the peppers though a sieve and return to the saucepan. Stir in the vinegar and sugar. Bring to a boil over medium heat, stirring constantly. Cook for 2 hours or until the mixture begins to thicken, stirring occasionally. Pour into half-pint canning jars or plastic food containers. Place lids on containers and let cool to room temperature. Store in the refrigerator. Serve over a block of cream cheese and serve with crackers.

Note: This jelly is also a good condiment with lamb or pork.

Yield: 12 half-pint jars

Green Chile Quiche

10 eggs
1/2 cup (1 stick) butter or margarine, melted
1/2 cup flour
1 teaspoon baking powder
1 teaspoon salt
2 cups cottage cheese
16 ounces Monterey Jack cheese, shredded
1 (8-ounce) can chopped green chiles

Beat the eggs in a mixing bowl for 4 to 5 minutes. Beat in the butter. Add the flour, baking powder and salt and beat until mixed. Fold in the cottage cheese, Monterey Jack cheese and green chiles. Spoon the mixture into an ungreased 9×13-inch baking dish. Bake at 450 degrees for 15 minutes. Reduce the oven temperature to 350 degrees and bake for 40 minutes or until golden brown. Cut into small squares and serve warm.

Yield: 15 servings

Hoisin Beef and Scallion Rolls

1/2 cup each soy sauce and vegetable oil
3 garlic cloves, minced
1/2 cup chopped fresh gingerroot
1/8 teaspoon freshly ground pepper, or to taste
1 (1-pound) London broil or flank steak, fat trimmed
1/2 cup hoisin sauce
White and pale green parts only of 1 bunch scallions, julienned

Combine the soy sauce, vegetable oil, garlic, gingerroot and pepper in a shallow dish and mix well. Add the steak and turn to coat. Marinate, covered, in the refrigerator for 24 hours, turning once. Remove the steak and pat dry. Discard the marinade. Broil the steak for 6 to 7 minutes per side for medium-rare. Let steak cool slightly and then freeze for 30 minutes for easier slicing. Place the steak on a cutting surface and thinly slice across the grain. Trim each slice to measure 2×4 inches. Brush hoisin sauce on each slice. Place a small bundle of julienned scallions on 1 end of each slice and roll securely. Arrange the rolls seam side down on a serving platter. Cover tightly and chill until serving time.

Yield: 40 servings

Shrimp Cocktail "Martini Style"

This recipe was provided by chef James Perillo.

8 cups chopped very ripe seedless watermelon
4 cups superfine sugar
1/4 cup light corn syrup
Juice of 1 lemon
2 cups finely chopped seeded peeled red tomatoes
2 cups finely chopped seedless watermelon
1 tablespoon finely chopped seeded fresh jalapeño chiles
3 scallions
1 tablespoon chopped fresh cilantro
1 tablespoon each Tabasco sauce and fresh lime juice
2 tablespoons olive oil blend (do not use extra-virgin olive oil)
Salt and pepper to taste
2 heads frisée lettuce or chicory
16 large cooked shrimp, peeled, deveined, chilled
8 each red and yellow teardrop tomatoes, halved
Sprigs of fresh cilantro

James Perillo

James Perillo is the Executive Chef of Caesar's Palace Hotel and Casino.

Purée 8 cups watermelon in batches in a food processor. Pour into a bowl. Add the sugar, corn syrup and lemon juice. Stir until the sugar dissolves. Pour the mixture into a freezer container. Freeze overnight. Process the frozen mixture in a food processor until slushy. Return to the freezer container and freeze for 2 hours. Mix the chopped tomatoes, 2 cups watermelon and jalapeño chiles in a bowl. Cut the green part off the scallions and reserve for garnish. Chop the remaining white part finely; add to the tomato mixture. Add the chopped cilantro, Tabasco sauce, lime juice and olive oil. Season with salt and pepper and toss to mix well. Cover and chill until serving time.

Rinse the lettuce in cold water. Separate leaves and pat dry. Place lettuce leaves in the bottom of 4 frozen martini glasses. Top with 1 tablespoon scoop of tomato mixture and 1 tablespoon scoop of watermelon sorbet. Place 4 shrimp around the rim of each glass. Garnish each with tomato halves, green part of scallions and cilantro sprigs.

NOTE: Shrimp Cocktail "Martini Style" is pictured on the cover.

Yield: 4 servings

Spinach Hors d'Oeuvre with Mustard Sauce

2 (10-ounce) packages frozen chopped spinach, thawed, drained
3/4 cup (1 1/2 sticks) butter, softened
6 eggs, beaten
2 cups herb-seasoned stuffing mix
1 cup freshly grated Parmesan cheese
Salt and pepper to taste
Mustard Sauce (below)

Squeeze any excess moisture from the spinach. Mix the spinach, butter, eggs, stuffing mix and Parmesan cheese in a bowl. Season with salt and pepper. Shape into 1-inch balls and place on a baking sheet. Bake at 375 degrees for 15 minutes. Serve with Mustard Sauce.

NOTE: These appetizers can be made ahead and frozen before baking. Freeze on a baking sheet and transfer to freezer bags when frozen. Thaw slightly before baking.

Yield: 10 servings

Mustard Sauce

1/2 cup dry mustard
1/2 cup white vinegar
1/4 cup sugar
1 egg yolk

Stir the dry mustard into the vinegar in a small bowl. Cover and let stand for several hours. Mix the sugar and egg yolk in a small saucepan. Stir in the mustard mixture. Cook over medium heat until thickened, stirring constantly. Remove from the heat and let cool to room temperature.

NOTE: The sauce can be made 1 to 2 days ahead. Cover and chill until needed.

Yield: about 1 cup

Tomatoes with Diced Mozzarella

16 ounces fresh mozzarella cheese
1 1/2 pounds cherry tomatoes
1/2 teaspoon minced garlic
1 tablespoon chopped fresh basil
1/2 teaspoon salt
1/4 teaspoon pepper, or to taste
1/4 cup olive oil

Cut the cheese into 1/2-inch cubes and place in a bowl. Cut the tomatoes into halves and add to the cheese. Whisk the garlic, basil, salt, pepper and olive oil in a small bowl. Pour over the cheese and tomatoes and stir gently to coat. Let stand for 2 hours at room temperature to blend flavors. Cover and chill. Serve with cocktail picks.

Yield: 8 servings

Ham and Swiss Appetizers

8 ounces Swiss cheese
8 ounces mozzarella cheese, shredded
8 ounces ricotta cheese
1 pound baked ham, chopped
2 eggs, beaten
1/8 teaspoon pepper
1 pound phyllo dough
1/2 cup (1 stick) butter, melted

Combine the Swiss cheese, mozzarella cheese, ricotta cheese, ham, eggs and pepper in a bowl and mix well. Prepare and fill the phyllo. Fold into triangles. (See pages 198 and 199 for directions on working with and shaping the phyllo.) Brush each triangle with melted butter. Place on a baking sheet. Bake at 350 degrees for 10 minutes or until golden brown. Remove to a wire rack to cool slightly. Serve warm.

VARIATION: You may substitute 16 ounces of drained, cooked, chopped spinach for the ham.

Yield: 4 dozen

Holiday Slush

1 quart each Hawaiian Punch, Squirt and cranberry juice cocktail
1 (12-ounce) can frozen orange juice concentrate, thawed
2 1/2 cups water
1 to 2 cups sugar
2 to 3 cups vodka or gin
1 to 2 cups rum

Mix the Hawaiian Punch, Squirt, cranberry juice cocktail, orange juice concentrate and water in a large bowl. Add the sugar, stirring until dissolved. Stir in the vodka and rum. Pour into a freezer container and freeze for 24 hours or longer. Allow to thaw for 1 hour for every 24 hours frozen. Three hours is the maximum thaw time even if frozen for longer than 72 hours. Stir before serving to make the mixture slushy.

Variation: Omit the water and combine all ingredients in a punch bowl. Fill bowl with ice.

Yield: 20 servings

Two-Cheese Tiropitas

2 tablespoons butter
1½ tablespoons flour
1 cup milk
2 eggs, beaten
½ cup grated Parmesan cheese
8 ounces feta cheese, crumbled
1 tablespoon chopped fresh parsley
Pepper to taste
1 pound phyllo dough
½ cup (1 stick) butter, melted

Melt 2 tablespoons butter in a saucepan over medium heat. Add the flour and stir until smooth. Reduce the heat. Stir in the milk gradually. Stir a small amount of the hot mixture into the beaten eggs; stir the eggs into the hot mixture. Cook until thickened, stirring constantly. Remove from the heat and let cool to room temperature. Stir in the Parmesan cheese, feta cheese and parsley. Season with pepper.

Prepare and fill the phyllo. Fold into triangles. (See pages 198 and 199 for directions on working with and shaping the phyllo.) Brush each tiropita with melted butter and place on a baking sheet. Bake at 375 degrees for 15 minutes or until golden brown. Remove to a wire rack and let cool slightly. Serve warm.

NOTE: These appetizers may also be frozen after they are brushed with melted butter but before they are baked. Do not thaw before baking.

Yield: 3 dozen

Artichoke Dip in Sourdough

1 bunch green onions, chopped
1 tablespoon minced garlic
1/2 cup (1 stick) butter, melted
12 ounces Cheddar cheese, shredded
8 ounces cream cheese, softened
2 cups sour cream
1 (14-ounce) can artichoke hearts, drained, chopped
1 round loaf sourdough bread
Cubes of French bread

Sauté the green onions and garlic in the butter in a saucepan until tender. Mix with the next 4 ingredients in a bowl. Remove the center portion of the bread, leaving the crust as a "bowl" for the filling. Spoon the artichoke filling into the bread bowl. Double wrap in foil and place on a baking sheet. Bake at 325 degrees for 1 1/2 hours or longer. Unwrap and place on a serving platter. Surround with the French bread cubes for dipping.

Yield: 6 to 8 servings

Tex-Mex Black Bean Dip

1 teaspoon vegetable oil
1/2 cup chopped onion
2 garlic cloves, minced
1 (15-ounce) can black beans, drained, slightly mashed
1/2 cup finely chopped tomato
1/3 cup mild picante sauce
1/2 teaspoon each cumin and chili powder
1/4 cup shredded Monterey Jack cheese
1/4 cup chopped fresh cilantro
1 tablespoon fresh lime juice

Heat the vegetable oil in a nonstick skillet. Add the onion and garlic. Sauté for 4 minutes or until tender. Add the beans, tomato, picante sauce, cumin and chili powder. Cook for 5 minutes or until thick, stirring constantly. Remove from the heat. Stir in the cheese, cilantro and lime juice. Spoon into a serving dish. Serve with tortilla chips.

Yield: about 2 cups

Slot Machines

The state of Nevada earns, on average, $27,600 per slot machine per year.

The world's largest regular slot machine, certified by the Guinness Book of World Records *and located at the Four Queens Hotel in downtown Las Vegas, is about the size of a small motor home. Six people can play it simultaneously.*

The largest slot machine payoff (approximately $39 million) occurred on a Megabucks machine in February 2000.

A 22-symbol, 3-reel slot machine has 10,648 combinations of symbols.

Slot machines account for 62 percent of all money won by Nevada casinos.

Slot machines contain from three to nine reels: crisscrossers, multiples, progressive, and specialty machines such as 21, keno, video poker, and horse or dog racing.

Chick-Pea Dip

2 (15-ounce) cans chick-peas, drained, rinsed
1/4 cup tahini
2 garlic cloves, minced
1/2 cup fresh lemon juice
1 teaspoon salt
1/2 teaspoon pepper
1/4 to 1/2 teaspoon cumin
1/4 cup water
2 tablespoons olive oil

Combine the chick-peas, tahini, garlic, lemon juice, salt, pepper, cumin, water and olive oil in a food processor container. Process until smooth. Pour into a serving dish. Garnish with additional olive oil, paprika and parsley. Serve with pita bread triangles.

Yield: about 2 cups

Peppered Bleu Cheese

8 ounces bleu cheese, crumbled
1/3 cup finely chopped red onion
1/4 cup chopped walnuts
3 tablespoons finely chopped fresh parsley
1/3 cup virgin olive oil
2 tablespoons cider vinegar
1/4 teaspoon cayenne pepper
1/2 teaspoon black pepper

Sprinkle the bleu cheese on the bottom of a quiche dish or pie plate. Layer the onion, walnuts and parsley over the cheese. Cover and chill until ready to serve.

Whisk the olive oil, vinegar, cayenne pepper and black pepper in a small bowl. Pour over the cheese mixture. Serve with nonsalty melba toast rounds, water crackers or baguette slices.

Yield: 12 servings

Cheddar Cheese Ball with Fruit Preserves

8 ounces sharp Cheddar cheese, shredded
8 ounces medium Cheddar cheese, shredded
1 small onion, grated
1 cup mayonnaise
1 teaspoon cayenne pepper
Strawberry preserves

Combine all the cheese, onion, mayonnaise and cayenne pepper in a bowl and mix well. Shape into a ball; make a well in the center. Place on a serving plate. Fill the well with preserves. Serve with crackers.

Yield: 12 to 16 servings

Olive Cheese Ball

8 ounces cream cheese, softened
4 ounces bleu cheese, crumbled
1/4 cup (1/2 stick) butter, softened
2/3 cup drained chopped black olives
1 tablespoon chopped fresh chives or green onions
1/3 cup chopped walnuts

Blend the cream cheese, bleu cheese and butter in a bowl. Stir in the olives and chives. Chill the mixture slightly. Shape into 3 balls and roll in the chopped walnuts to coat. Wrap in plastic wrap and chill until firm. Serve with assorted crackers.

Yield: 30 to 40 servings

Melted Brie with Winter Fruit

3/4 cup chopped pitted dates
1 small apple, peeled, cored, chopped
1 small firm pear, peeled, cored, chopped
1/2 cup currants or raisins
1/2 cup chopped pecans
1/3 cup rosé wine or apple juice
1 (16-ounce) wheel of Brie cheese, well chilled
Thin baguette slices

Combine the dates, apple, pear, currants, pecans and wine in a small bowl and mix well. Let stand for 2 hours.

Place the Brie on a cutting surface. Slice into halves horizontally. Place the bottom half cut side up in a shallow round 10-inch baking dish. Spread with 2 1/2 cups of the fruit mixture. Cover with the top half of the Brie, cut side down. Spoon the remaining fruit onto the center of the Brie.

Bake at 350 degrees for 25 to 30 minutes or until the cheese melts at the edges and the center is warm. Place on a hot plate to keep warm. Spread on baguette slices.

NOTE: This spread can be made up to 2 days ahead before baking. Cover and chill.

Yield: 16 servings

Chutney Cheese Balls

This was the most popular appetizer in our first cookbook, Winning at the Table (1985).

24 ounces cream cheese, softened
1 cup sour cream
1 cup chopped raisins
1 cup chopped salted peanuts
8 slices bacon, crisp-cooked, crumbled
1/2 cup chopped green onions
4 teaspoons curry powder
Chutney
Flaked coconut
Finely chopped fresh parsley

Mix the cream cheese, sour cream, raisins, peanuts, bacon, green onions and curry powder in a bowl. Shape the mixture into 2 balls and wrap each in plastic wrap. Chill until firm. Unwrap and place on serving plates. Top with chutney, coconut and parsley. Serve with crackers.

NOTE: The cheese balls may be made ahead and frozen for up to 3 months. Thaw for 2 to 3 hours before topping with the chutney, coconut and parsley.

Yield: 20 to 30 servings

Baked Almond and Crab Appetizer

8 ounces cream cheese, softened
6 ounces crab meat, flaked
2 tablespoons finely chopped onion
1 tablespoon cream-style horseradish
1/4 teaspoon salt
1/8 teaspoon pepper, or to taste
1/3 cup slivered almonds

Mix the cream cheese, crab meat, onion, horseradish, salt and pepper in a bowl. Spoon into a greased 8-inch pie plate. Sprinkle the almonds on top. Bake at 375 degrees for 15 minutes. Serve with crackers.

Yield: 12 servings

Warm Crab Dip

16 ounces cream cheese, softened
1 cup mayonnaise
2 teaspoons Dijon mustard
4 teaspoons prepared horseradish
1 tablespoon dried onion flakes
1 teaspoon seasoned salt
1 teaspoon garlic powder
1 teaspoon parsley flakes
16 ounces flake-style imitation crab meat

Combine the cream cheese, mayonnaise, Dijon mustard, horseradish, onion flakes, seasoned salt, garlic powder and parsley flakes in a bowl and mix well. Fold in the imitation crab meat and mix gently. Spoon the mixture into a 9-inch round quiche pan. Bake at 375 degrees for 20 to 25 minutes or just until bubbly. Serve warm with assorted crackers.

NOTE: This recipe may be halved.

Yield: 18 to 20 servings

Tasty Crab Spread

24 ounces cream cheese, softened
1/2 cup mayonnaise
2 teaspoons prepared mustard
2 teaspoons onion juice
2 teaspoons confectioners' sugar
Garlic salt to taste
Seasoning salt to taste
12 ounces crab meat, flaked

Combine the cream cheese, mayonnaise, mustard, onion juice, confectioners' sugar, garlic salt and seasoning salt in a food processor container. Process until smooth. Stir in the crab meat. Spoon into a serving dish. Cover and chill. Serve with crackers or baguette slices.

Yield: 20 servings

Pâté Maison

2 quarts water
2 teaspoons peppercorns
2 teaspoons whole cloves
3 bay leaves
Few sprigs of parsley
2 1/2 pounds chicken livers
1 pound (4 sticks) butter, softened
1 small onion, finely chopped
1 large garlic clove, minced
1 tablespoon salt
2 teaspoons dry mustard
1/2 teaspoon freshly ground nutmeg
1/8 teaspoon hot pepper sauce, or to taste
1/2 cup heavy cream
1/4 cup brandy

Combine the water, peppercorns, cloves, bay leaves and parsley in a
4-quart saucepan. Bring to a boil and simmer for 10 minutes. Strain
through a sieve and return the liquid to the saucepan. Discard the spices.
Add the chicken livers to the liquid and cook, just below a simmer, for
10 minutes or until the liquid is clear and rosy and the chicken livers are
done. Drain the chicken livers and grind in a meat grinder or purée
in a food processor.

Mix the butter, onion, garlic, salt, dry mustard, nutmeg, pepper sauce and
heavy cream in a large bowl. Add the chicken liver purée and mix well.
Stir in the brandy.

Line a 5×9-inch loaf pan with foil. Spoon the pâté into the loaf pan and
press with a spoon to pack it down. Cover and chill thoroughly. Invert
the loaf pan on a serving plate and remove the foil.

NOTE: Chill the pâté overnight for the flavors to fully develop.

Yield: 12 servings

Spinach Artichoke Spread

2 (8-ounce) cans artichoke hearts, drained, chopped
1/2 cup freshly grated Parmesan cheese
1/2 cup shredded pepper Jack cheese
3/4 cup sour cream
1/4 cup mayonnaise
8 ounces cream cheese, softened
3 to 4 garlic cloves, minced
1 (10-ounce) package frozen chopped spinach, thawed,
    drained, squeezed dry
Green part only of 2 to 3 green onions, chopped

Combine the artichoke hearts, Parmesan cheese, pepper Jack
cheese, sour cream, mayonnaise, cream cheese, garlic, spinach
and green onions in a bowl. Stir until mixed.

Spoon the artichoke mixture into a shallow baking dish and bake
at 325 degrees for 30 to 45 minutes or until the top is lightly
browned. Serve hot with tortilla chips or crackers.

VARIATION: Add 1 to 2 seeded and finely chopped jalapeño
chiles to the mixture for some extra zest.

Yield: 12 servings

Walnut Dill Dip

1 cucumber, peeled,
*   seeded, finely chopped*
1/2 teaspoon salt
2 1/2 cups plain yogurt
4 teaspoons finely chopped
*   fresh dill*
1 small green chile, seeded,
*   finely chopped*
1/2 cup coarsely chopped
*   walnuts*
2 tablespoons golden
*   raisins*

Place the chopped cucumber
in a sieve and sprinkle with
the salt. Let drain for
30 minutes. Do not rinse.
Pat dry with paper towels.
Beat the yogurt in a bowl
until smooth. Stir in the
drained cucumber, dill, green
chile, walnuts and raisins.
Spoon into a serving bowl
and garnish with additional
dill. Serve with pita chips or
Belgian endive.

Note: You can add 1/4 cup of
crumbled bleu cheese to add
some zing to this dip.

Yield: 6 servings

Walnut Salmon Logs

8 ounces cream cheese, softened
2 tablespoons finely chopped onion
1 teaspoon liquid smoke
1½ to 2 teaspoons prepared horseradish
1 tablespoon fresh lemon juice
1 pound cooked salmon, skin and bones removed
1 cup chopped walnuts
1 bunch fresh parsley, finely chopped

Mix the cream cheese, onion, liquid smoke, horseradish and lemon juice in a bowl. Add the salmon and mix well. Cover and chill for 2 hours. Divide the mixture into 2 equal portions on a work surface. Shape each into a log. Roll in the walnuts and parsley. Wrap each log in plastic wrap and chill until firm. Serve with crackers.

NOTE: The logs can be made ahead and frozen. Thaw in the refrigerator before serving.

Yield: 6 to 10 servings

Brie Soup

¼ cup (½ stick) butter
½ cup chopped onion
½ cup thinly sliced celery
¼ cup flour
2 cups milk
2 cups chicken broth
12 ounces Brie cheese with rind, cubed
Salt and pepper to taste

Melt the butter in a saucepan. Add the onion and celery and sauté under tender. Stir in the flour and remove from the heat. Whisk in the milk and chicken broth. Return to the heat and simmer until thick, stirring constantly. Add the cheese and simmer until the cheese is melted, stirring constantly. Remove from the heat and purée in batches in a food processor or blender. Season with salt and pepper. Return to the saucepan and heat until very hot but not boiling. Ladle into 4 bowls. Garnish with chopped chives. Serve with French bread.

Yield: 4 servings

Autumn Bisque

2 tablespoons butter
2 carrots, peeled, sliced
1 onion, chopped
1 rib celery, chopped
2 to 2¹/₂ pounds butternut squash, peeled, seeded, cubed
2 potatoes, peeled, cubed
5 to 6 cups chicken broth
1 to 1¹/₂ teaspoons curry powder
¹/₈ teaspoon nutmeg, or to taste
¹/₈ teaspoon ginger, or to taste

Melt the butter in a large saucepan. Add the carrots, onion and celery and sauté until tender. Stir in the squash, potatoes and chicken broth. Bring to a simmer and simmer for 40 minutes. Stir in the curry powder, nutmeg and ginger and remove from the heat.

Purée the soup in small batches in a food processor or blender. Return to the saucepan and reheat gently. Add more chicken broth if the soup is too thick. Ladle into 6 bowls. Garnish with chopped apple and sour cream.

Yield: 6 servings

Winter Weather Menu

Autumn Bisque (at left)

Baked Goat Cheese Salad (page 46)

Green Beans with Mustard Vinaigrette (page 84)

Garlic Cream Cheese Mashed Potatoes (page 88)

Pork Tenderloin with Rosemary (page 110)

Five-Flavor Pound Cake (page 156)

Chicken Broccoli Soup

$^{1}/_{2}$ cup finely chopped carrots
$^{1}/_{2}$ cup finely chopped onion
$^{1}/_{2}$ cup finely chopped celery
1 cup finely chopped broccoli stems
$1^{1}/_{2}$ teaspoons dried thyme
$1^{1}/_{2}$ teaspoons dried oregano
1 teaspoon dried basil
$^{1}/_{2}$ cup dry white wine
8 to 16 ounces chicken breasts, cooked, cubed
4 cups chicken broth
1 (15-ounce) can black beans, drained
1 (12-ounce) can evaporated skim milk
$1^{1}/_{2}$ cups broccoli florets
1 tablespoon Worcestershire sauce
1 teaspoon Tabasco sauce

Spray the bottom of a stockpot with nonstick cooking spray. Add the
carrots, onion, celery and broccoli stems. Sauté over medium heat for
5 minutes. Stir in the thyme, oregano, basil and wine. Simmer for
15 minutes or until the liquid is reduced by $^{1}/_{2}$.

Add the cubed chicken, chicken broth and beans to the mixture in the
stockpot. Cook over low heat for 3 to 5 minutes or until heated through.
Stir in the evaporated milk and broccoli florets. Cook for 5 minutes,
stirring constantly to prevent the soup from boiling. Stir in the
Worcestershire sauce and Tabasco sauce and cook for 2 minutes.

VARIATION: Try using smoked, barbecued or roasted chicken in this
soup for a different flavor.

Yield: 4 to 6 servings

Chili Blanco

1 pound dried large white beans
6 cups (or more) chicken broth
2 garlic cloves, minced
1 medium onion, chopped
1 tablespoon vegetable oil
1 medium onion, chopped
2 (4-ounce) cans chopped green chiles
2 teaspoons cumin
1 1/2 teaspoons dried oregano
1/4 teaspoon ground cloves
1/4 teaspoon cayenne pepper
4 cups chopped cooked chicken breast
3 cups shredded Monterey Jack cheese
Salsa Cruda (at right)

Sort and rinse the beans. Combine the beans, chicken broth, garlic and 1 chopped onion in a large saucepan. Bring to a boil. Reduce the heat and simmer for at least 3 hours or until the beans are very soft. Add more chicken broth if needed.

Heat the vegetable oil in a skillet. Add 1 chopped onion and sauté until tender. Stir in the green chiles, cumin, oregano, cloves and cayenne pepper. Add to the bean mixture. Stir in the chicken and simmer for 1 hour. Spoon into bowls and top with the cheese and Salsa Cruda.

NOTE: For a buffet, offer some or all of the following condiments: chopped tomatoes, chopped parsley, chopped black olives, guacamole, chopped green onions, sour cream, crumbled tortilla chips and Salsa Cruda.

Yield: 6 to 8 servings

Salsa Cruda

*2 cups drained
chopped canned
Italian tomatoes
2 tablespoons red
wine vinegar
1/2 cup finely chopped
onion
1 to 2 canned or fresh
serrano chiles,
finely chopped
1 tablespoon chopped
fresh coriander
Salt and pepper to taste*

Mix the tomatoes, vinegar, onion, chiles and coriander in a bowl. Season with salt and pepper. Cover and chill thoroughly.

Yield: 2 1/2 cups

Creamy Corn Chowder

4 slices bacon
1 medium onion, finely chopped
3 ribs celery, finely chopped
5 cups chicken broth
2 large russet potatoes, peeled, cut into 1/2-inch cubes
1 bay leaf
1/2 teaspoon thyme
3 cups fresh or frozen whole kernel corn
2 cups heavy cream
Salt and freshly ground pepper to taste
Tabasco sauce to taste

Cook the bacon in a skillet until crisp. Remove to paper towels to drain. Measure 2 tablespoons of the bacon drippings and place in a 4-quart saucepan. Add the onion and celery and sauté until tender but not browned. Add the chicken broth, potatoes, bay leaf and thyme. Bring to a boil and reduce the heat. Simmer for 30 minutes or until the potatoes are tender.

Mash some of the potatoes in the soup with a potato masher. Stir in the corn and cook for 5 to 10 minutes. Add the cream and cook over low heat until heated through, stirring occasionally. Do not boil. Season with salt, pepper and Tabasco sauce. Ladle into bowls. Sprinkle with the bacon. Garnish with chopped fresh dill.

NOTE: For lighter fare, substitute half-and-half, milk or evaporated milk for the heavy cream.

Yield: 6 servings

Tawny Port Lentil Soup

1/4 cup extra-virgin olive oil
2 to 4 carrots, peeled, chopped
White part only of 2 leeks, chopped
2 to 4 ribs celery, chopped
4 to 6 garlic cloves, minced
1 large red onion, chopped
1 (28-ounce) can tomatoes, or 3 1/2 cups chopped
    peeled fresh tomatoes
8 cups water
Salt and pepper to taste
1/2 cup tawny port or sherry
1 1/2 cups red or green lentils
Grated pecorino cheese

Heat the olive oil in an 8- to 10-quart stockpot. Add the carrots, leeks, celery, garlic and onion and sauté until tender but not browned. Stir in the tomatoes and water and season with salt and pepper.

Bring the soup to a simmer and stir in the port. Simmer for 20 to 30 minutes. Stir in the lentils and simmer for 40 to 50 minutes or until lentils are tender but not mushy. Add more water if needed. Ladle into bowls and top with cheese.

Yield: 8 to 10 servings

Gaming Trivia

There are 4,350 live table games in Nevada.

The state of Nevada wins on average $2.8 billion for live table games (blackjack, poker, etc.).

The annual gross gaming revenue topped $8.1 billion in 1998.

Most of the gaming taxes collected by the state are channeled into public education in Nevada.

The Las Vegas metropolitan area, which attracts 30 million visitors annually, accounts for the lion's share of Nevada winnings.

Tourism's yearly economic impact on Las Vegas is approximately $25 billion.

The games visitors play most frequently are slot machines (52%) and blackjack (17%). Eleven percent of visitors do not gamble at all.

French Onion Soup

3 tablespoons butter
3 large onions, thinly sliced
1 tablespoon flour
1/2 teaspoon salt
Freshly ground pepper to taste
5 cups beef broth
4 slices French or Italian bread
1/4 cup grated Parmesan cheese
1/4 cup shredded Swiss cheese

Melt the butter in a heavy saucepan. Add the onions and cook over low heat until golden brown, stirring occasionally. Sprinkle the flour over the onions and cook for a few minutes, stirring constantly. Add the salt and season with pepper. Stir in the beef broth and bring to a boil. Reduce the heat. Simmer, partially covered, for 30 minutes.

Toast the bread slices and place in a large ovenproof soup tureen or 4 individual ovenproof bowls. Sprinkle the Parmesan cheese over the bread. Ladle the soup over the bread and sprinkle with the Swiss cheese. Place under a preheated broiler and broil until the cheese is golden brown. Serve immediately.

Yield: 4 servings

Creamy Onion and Potato Soup

1 tablespoon butter
White part only of 1 bunch leeks, chopped
2 tablespoons butter
1 large onion, chopped
1 garlic clove, minced
2 tablespoons flour
2 (14-ounce) cans chicken broth
3 large Yukon gold potatoes, peeled, cubed
Salt and pepper to taste
1 cup milk

Melt 1 tablespoon butter in a skillet. Add the leeks and sauté until tender. Remove from the heat and set aside.

Melt 2 tablespoons butter in a large saucepan. Add the onion and garlic and sauté until tender. Add the flour and cook for a few minutes, stirring constantly. Stir in the chicken broth gradually. Add the potatoes and cooked leeks and season with salt and pepper. Cook for 20 to 30 minutes or until the potatoes are tender. Remove from the heat.

Purée 1/2 to 3/4 of the soup in a blender. Return the puréed soup to the saucepan. Stir in the milk and cook until heated through. Ladle into bowls. Garnish with shredded Cheddar cheese and chopped green onions.

Yield: 4 to 6 servings

Strip Trivia

Gambling was legalized in Nevada in 1931.

Howard Hughes moved to the Desert Inn in 1966.

The world-famous inexpensive Las Vegas buffet debuted at the original El Rancho in the early 1940s.

There were approximately 130,000 hotel rooms by the end of the year 2000.

The world's tallest, brightest, and most elaborate signs announce the ultimate in entertainment choices, ranging from close encounters to multimillion dollar spectacular production shows.

Visitors arrive by car (41%), air (44%), bus (8%), RV (6%), and train (0.4%).

There are an estimated 15,000 miles of neon tubing in the signs on the Las Vegas Strip.

March is the busiest month for tourism in Las Vegas. Except for Christmas and New Year's, December is the slowest month.

Sweet Red Pepper Bisque

3 tablespoons butter
3 small yellow onions, sliced
12 red bell peppers, seeded, cut into thin strips
3 tomatoes, cut into quarters
6 tablespoons uncooked white rice
6 tablespoons Cognac
9 cups chicken broth
$1^1/_2$ cups heavy cream
$^1/_8$ teaspoon cayenne pepper
Salt and black pepper to taste
3 tablespoons chopped fresh parsley
$^3/_4$ teaspoon paprika

Melt the butter in a large saucepan. Add the onions and sauté until translucent. Add the bell peppers and tomatoes and cook over medium-high heat for 15 minutes, stirring frequently. Stir in the rice and cook for 10 minutes. Stir in the Cognac and cook for 5 minutes. Add the chicken broth and bring to a boil. Reduce the heat and simmer for 20 minutes. Add the cream and simmer for 20 minutes.

Remove from the heat and purée the soup in batches in a food processor or blender. Strain through a sieve and return to the saucepan. Stir in the cayenne pepper and season with salt and black pepper. Ladle into bowls and top with chopped parsley and paprika.

NOTE: This soup can be made 2 to 3 days ahead. Cover and chill. Reheat gently before serving.

Yield: 10 to 12 servings

Tomato Mint Soup

2 (28-ounce) cans chopped tomatoes
3 (28-ounce) cans chicken broth
5 small zucchini (about 1 1/2 pounds), quartered lengthwise,
    cut into 1/2-inch pieces
6 large garlic cloves, minced
1/4 cup dried mint
1 teaspoon salt
3/4 teaspoon pepper
1/8 to 1/4 teaspoon Tabasco sauce (optional)
1/2 cup small-shape pasta

Combine the tomatoes, chicken broth, zucchini, garlic, mint, salt, pepper and Tabasco sauce in a large saucepan. Bring to a boil. Reduce the heat and simmer for 30 minutes or until the zucchini is tender. Add the pasta and simmer for 5 minutes or until the pasta is al dente.

Yield: 6 to 8 servings

Zucchini Soup

1 pound zucchini
1 (10-ounce) can chicken broth
1/2 cup chopped green onions
1/2 cup dry white wine
2 tablespoons butter
1/2 teaspoon salt

Trim the zucchini. Finely chop the unpeeled zucchini. Combine the zucchini, chicken broth and green onions in a saucepan. Cook until tender. Let cool slightly and purée in a blender with the wine, butter and salt. Return the puréed zucchini to the saucepan. Cook over low heat until hot but not boiling. Thin with additional chicken broth if desired.

NOTE: This soup can be made up to 2 days ahead. Cover and chill. Reheat gently.

Yield: 4 servings

Climate

Las Vegas sits in a "bowl" surrounded by mountains on all four sides: The Sheep Range to the north, the Frenchman to the east, the Spring Mountain Range to the west, and the McCullough Range to the south. Las Vegas averages 294 days of sunshine per year (211 clear and 83 partly cloudy). Hot summers and moderate winters along with low humidity combine with ideal spring and fall temperatures to make Las Vegas an excellent year-round place to live or vacation. The temperature ranges from 28 degrees Fahrenheit in the winter to 117 degrees in the summer. The wind blows more than 300 days per year. It averages 9.3 miles per hour, with 90 miles per hour being the highest gust ever recorded.

Cabbage Salad with Mint Dressing

1/2 cup olive oil
1/2 cup lemon juice
1 tablespoon dried mint
1 to 2 garlic cloves, minced (optional)
1/2 teaspoon salt
1/4 teaspoon pepper
1 medium head cabbage, shredded

Whisk the olive oil, lemon juice, mint, garlic, salt and pepper in a bowl. Place the cabbage in a large bowl. Add the dressing and toss to coat. Cover and chill.

VARIATION: Try Creamy Mint Dressing (below) for a slightly different slaw.

Yield: 8 servings

Creamy Mint Dressing

1/2 cup olive oil
1/2 cup white vinegar
1/2 cup mayonnaise
1 tablespoon dried mint
1 to 2 garlic cloves, minced (optional)
1/2 teaspoon salt
1/4 teaspoon pepper

Combine the olive oil, vinegar, mayonnaise, mint, garlic, salt and pepper in a jar with a tight-fitting lid. Shake until mixed well.

Yield: 8 servings

Red Rock Picnic Slaw

    1 medium head cabbage, shredded
    2 ribs celery, finely chopped
    2 carrots, peeled, finely chopped
    2 medium red onions, finely chopped
    1 green bell pepper, finely chopped
    1 1/2 cups sugar
    Cider Vinaigrette (at right)

Combine the cabbage, celery, carrots, onions, bell pepper and sugar in a large bowl. Add the hot Cider Vinaigrette. Toss to coat and allow to cool to room temperature. Cover and chill for 1 day or longer.

NOTE: This salad stays crisp and flavorful in the refrigerator for up to 1 week.

    Yield: 8 to 10 servings

Cider Vinaigrette

1 cup vegetable oil
1 cup cider vinegar
2 tablespoons salt
2 tablespoons sugar

Combine the vegetable oil, vinegar, salt and sugar in a saucepan. Bring to a boil over medium heat, stirring constantly.

Yield: about 2 cups

Broccoli Salad

    1 1/2 pounds broccoli, trimmed, cut into bite-size pieces
    6 slices bacon, crisp-cooked, crumbled
    1/2 cup raisins
    1/4 cup chopped onion
    1/2 cup sunflower seed kernels
    1/2 cup slivered almonds
    1 cup mayonnaise
    1/4 cup sugar
    2 tablespoons vinegar

Cook the broccoli in a small amount of boiling water in a saucepan until tender-crisp. Submerge in ice water to chill. Drain and place in a bowl. Add the bacon, raisins, onion, sunflower seeds and almonds and toss to mix. Cover and chill for 1 hour.

Combine the mayonnaise, sugar and vinegar in a small bowl. Stir until the sugar dissolves. Add to the broccoli mixture and toss to coat. This salad keeps well in the refrigerator for several days.

    Yield: 6 to 8 servings

Feta and Walnut Salad

    8 to 10 cups mixed salad greens
    12 medium mushrooms, sliced
    1 small cucumber, cut lengthwise into strips
    1/2 cup chopped walnuts
    4 ounces feta cheese, crumbled
    1 small Bermuda onion, thinly sliced
    2 tomatoes, cut into wedges
    Herbal Dijon Vinaigrette (below)

Combine the salad greens, mushrooms, cucumber, walnuts, cheese, onion and tomatoes in a large bowl and toss to mix well. Add the Herbal Dijon Vinaigrette and toss gently.

VARIATION: For a main dish salad, top each serving with strips of grilled chicken breast.

    Yield: 8 servings

Herbal Dijon Vinaigrette

    1/2 cup canola oil
    1/2 cup olive oil
    1/3 cup balsamic vinegar
    3 garlic cloves, minced
    1/4 teaspoon salt
    1 tablespoon Dijon mustard
    1/8 teaspoon pepper
    2 tablespoons chopped fresh parsley
    2 tablespoons chopped fresh basil
    1 teaspoon chopped fresh rosemary

Whisk the canola oil, olive oil and vinegar in a bowl until mixed. Add the garlic, salt, Dijon mustard, pepper, parsley, basil and rosemary and whisk until mixed. Best if prepared 1 day in advance.

NOTE: This vinaigrette keeps well in the refrigerator.

    Yield: about 1 1/3 cups

Caesar Salad

4 cups torn romaine lettuce
2 cups iceberg lettuce chunks
1 cup thinly sliced red onion
1/2 cup pitted black olives
2 hard-cooked eggs, finely chopped
1/2 cup Italian Dressing (below)
1/2 teaspoon salt
1/8 teaspoon pepper, or to taste
1/3 cup grated Parmesan cheese
Parmesan Croutons (at right)

Combine all the lettuce, onion, olives and eggs in a large bowl. Add the Italian Dressing, salt and pepper and toss to coat. Add the Parmesan cheese and croutons and toss gently.

NOTE: You may use bottled Italian dressing if desired.

Yield: 6 to 8 servings

Italian Dressing

1/4 cup balsamic vinegar
3/4 cup olive oil
2 teaspoons Dijon mustard
1 teaspoon Worcestershire sauce
2 tablespoons finely chopped fresh basil, or
    1 tablespoon dried basil
1 tablespoon minced garlic

Combine the vinegar, olive oil, Dijon mustard, Worcestershire sauce, basil and garlic in a jar with a tight-fitting lid. Shake until mixed well.

NOTE: This dressing keeps well in the refrigerator for several days.

Yield: about 1 cup

Parmesan Croutons

*2 cups seasoned Italian
  bread cubes
3 tablespoons Italian
  Dressing (at left)
2 tablespoons grated
  Parmesan cheese*

*Place the bread cubes
in a bowl. Add the Italian
Dressing and Parmesan
cheese and toss to coat.
Spread the bread cubes
in a single layer in a
shallow baking pan. Bake
at 400 degrees for 8 to
10 minutes or until lightly
browned. Stir occasionally
while baking.*

Yield: 2 cups

Baked Goat Cheese Salad

1 cup fine bread crumbs
1/4 teaspoon pepper
1 (8-ounce) cylinder goat cheese, chilled
Olive oil
6 cups mixed salad greens
1/2 cup fresh raspberries
1 cup chopped pecans
Raspberry Vinaigrette (below)

Mix the bread crumbs and pepper in a shallow bowl. Slice the cheese into 1/2-inch rounds. Dip the cheese rounds in olive oil and then in the bread crumbs and turn to coat. Place the coated cheese rounds on a lightly oiled baking sheet. Chill for 10 minutes. Bake at 400 degrees for 5 minutes or until lightly browned and beginning to bubble. Remove to a wire rack to cool slightly.

Combine the salad greens, raspberries and pecans in a bowl. Add the Raspberry Vinaigrette and toss lightly. Arrange the salad on plates; top with the warm cheese rounds.

Yield: 4 to 6 servings

Raspberry Vinaigrette

1/2 cup olive oil
3 tablespoons raspberry vinegar
1/4 teaspoon vanilla extract
1/4 teaspoon salt
2 teaspoons finely chopped fresh thyme

Whisk the olive oil, vinegar, vanilla, salt and thyme in a small bowl until mixed well.

Yield: 3/4 cup

Mixed Greens with Sugared Almonds

1 head Bibb lettuce, torn into bite-size pieces
1 head leaf lettuce, torn into bite-size pieces
1 (11-ounce) can mandarin oranges, drained
10 fresh strawberries, hulled, thinly sliced
1 green onion, chopped
Poppy Seed Dressing (below)
Sugared Almonds (at right)

Combine all the lettuce, mandarin oranges, strawberries and green onion in a large bowl. Toss gently to mix. Add the Poppy Seed Dressing and toss gently. Arrange the salad on individual plates and sprinkle with Sugared Almonds.

Yield: 6 servings

Poppy Seed Dressing

$1/2$ cup sugar
1 tablespoon poppy seeds
2 tablespoons sesame seeds
$1^1/2$ teaspoons minced onion
$1/4$ teaspoon paprika
$1/4$ cup cider vinegar
$1/4$ cup wine vinegar
$1/2$ cup vegetable oil

Whisk the sugar, poppy seeds, sesame seeds, onion, paprika, cider vinegar, wine vinegar and vegetable oil in a small bowl until mixed well.

Yield: $1^1/2$ cups

Sugared Almonds

1 egg white, at room
   temperature
$1/4$ cup sugar
1 cup slivered almonds
2 tablespoons butter,
   melted

Beat the egg white in a small bowl with an electric mixer until foamy. Add the sugar gradually, beating constantly at high speed until stiff peaks form. Fold the almonds into the beaten egg white. Pour the melted butter into a 9×9-inch baking pan and tilt the pan to coat the bottom. Spread the almonds over the melted butter. Bake at 325 degrees for 20 to 25 minutes or until the almonds are dry, stirring every 5 minutes. Set aside and let the almonds cool completely.

Yield: 1 cup

Mandarin Orange and Almond Salad

1 head romaine lettuce, torn into bite-size pieces
1 (11-ounce) can mandarin oranges, drained
1/2 cup thinly sliced red onion
Red Wine Vinaigrette (below)
1/2 cup slivered almonds, toasted

Combine the lettuce, mandarin oranges and onion in a large bowl. Add the Red Wine Vinaigrette and toss to coat. Top with the almonds.

Yield: 6 servings

Red Wine Vinaigrette

1/2 cup olive oil
3 tablespoons red wine vinegar
1 tablespoon lemon juice
2 tablespoons sugar
1/2 teaspoon salt
1/2 teaspoon dry mustard
1/2 teaspoon grated onion
1/8 teaspoon almond extract

Whisk the olive oil, vinegar, lemon juice, sugar, salt, dry mustard, onion and almond extract in a small bowl until mixed. Cover and chill for 1 hour.

Yield: about 3/4 cup

Country Club Salad

24 ounces baby spinach leaves
3 radishes, thinly sliced
1 medium red onion, thinly sliced
8 ounces feta cheese, crumbled
2 (11-ounce) cans mandarin oranges, drained
1 cup chopped walnuts or cashews
Honey Lemon Dressing (below)

Combine the spinach, radishes, onion, cheese, mandarin oranges and walnuts in a large bowl. Add enough Honey Lemon Dressing to coat and toss lightly.

NOTE: Grilled chicken or shrimp can be added to make this a main course salad.

Yield: 8 servings

Honey Lemon Dressing

1 cup vegetable oil
1/2 cup sugar
1/2 cup honey
6 tablespoons tarragon vinegar
3 tablespoons lemon juice
1 teaspoon grated onion
1 teaspoon dry mustard
1 teaspoon paprika
1 teaspoon salt
1 teaspoon curry powder (optional)

Whisk the vegetable oil, sugar, honey, vinegar, lemon juice, onion, dry mustard, paprika, salt and curry powder in a bowl until mixed.

NOTE: Try using balsamic vinegar instead of tarragon vinegar for a different flavor. Any remaining dressing can be stored, covered, in the refrigerator for up to 1 month.

Yield: about 2 1/2 cups

Lunch with the Girls Menu

Citrus Iced Tea (page 57)

Tomato Mint Soup (page 41)

Country Club Salad (at left)

Passion Fruit Syllabub (page 192)

Roasted Pepper and Artichoke Salad

4 large red bell peppers
1 (6-ounce) jar marinated artichoke hearts, drained
1/4 cup balsamic vinegar
1/2 cup olive oil
2 scallions, finely chopped
1/4 cup finely chopped fresh basil
Salt and pepper to taste
4 ounces feta cheese, crumbled

Roast the bell peppers directly over a gas flame or under the broiler until evenly charred. Place in a paper bag and let stand for 10 minutes. Peel and seed the peppers; cut into 1/2-inch strips. Place in a medium glass bowl. Cut the artichoke hearts into quarters and add to the peppers.

Whisk the vinegar, olive oil, scallions and basil in a bowl. Season with salt and pepper. Slowly drizzle over the pepper mixture while whisking. Add the feta cheese and toss gently to coat. Remove to a serving platter and serve with baguette rounds or crackers.

NOTE: Try using 2 red and 2 yellow bell peppers for a different look.

Yield: 4 servings

Red and Green Holiday Salad

This salad is pictured on page 12.

10 cups torn spinach leaves
1 avocado, pitted, thinly sliced
Seeds of 1 pomegranate
1 cup Champagne Vinaigrette (below)

Place the spinach leaves in a large salad bowl. Arrange the avocado slices around the outside edge. Place the pomegranate seeds in the center of the salad. Add the warm Champagne Vinaigrette and toss to mix. Serve on salad plates.

NOTE: Even if pomegranates are out of season or unavailable, this is still a delicious salad.

Yield: 8 servings

Champagne Vinaigrette

1 cup Champagne vinegar
1 tablespoon sugar
2 teaspoons dry vermouth
1 teaspoon Dijon mustard
2 cups olive oil
Salt and pepper to taste

Combine the vinegar, sugar, vermouth and Dijon mustard in a saucepan. Heat over medium heat until simmering. Whisk in the olive oil in a thin steady stream. Season with salt and pepper. Remove from heat and use warm.

Yield: 3 cups

Spinach Salad with Chili Dressing

4 bunches spinach, torn into bite-size pieces
4 hard-cooked eggs, sliced
1 large red onion, thinly sliced
Italian-seasoned croutons
Chili Dressing (below)

Combine the spinach, eggs, onion and croutons in a large bowl. Add the Chili Dressing and toss gently to mix.

Yield: 8 servings

Chili Dressing

2 tablespoons finely chopped celery
1 tablespoon finely chopped white onion
1 tablespoon finely chopped bell pepper
1 tablespoon finely chopped fresh parsley
1/4 cup chili sauce
1/2 cup ketchup
3/4 cup vegetable oil
1/4 cup red wine vinegar
1/3 cup sugar
1/2 teaspoon Worcestershire sauce
1/4 teaspoon dry mustard
1/4 teaspoon dried oregano
Salt to taste

Purée the celery, onion, pepper and parsley in a food processor. Pour into a bowl. Add the chili sauce, ketchup, vegetable oil, vinegar, sugar, Worcestershire sauce, dry mustard and oregano. Whisk until mixed. Season with salt. Cover and chill for 2 days.

Yield: about 2 cups

Summer Spinach Salad

1 bunch spinach
1¹/₂ cups strawberries, hulled, sliced
1 small red onion, thinly sliced
¹/₃ cup sesame seeds, toasted
Balsamic Dijon Vinaigrette (below)

Tear the spinach into bite-size pieces. Combine the spinach, strawberries, onion and sesame seeds in a bowl and toss gently to mix. Add the Balsamic Dijon Vinaigrette and toss to mix well.

Yield: 4 to 6 servings

Balsamic Dijon Vinaigrette

¹/₄ cup balsamic vinegar
¹/₄ cup rice vinegar
2 tablespoons Dijon mustard
2 tablespoons honey

Mix the balsamic vinegar with the rice vinegar in a bowl. Add the Dijon mustard and honey and whisk until mixed.

Yield: about ³/₄ cup

Winter Spinach Salad

6 ounces baby spinach leaves
$1/2$ cup dried cranberries
$1/2$ cup chopped almonds, preferably honey roasted
1 cup chopped unpeeled red apple
Honey Mustard Vinaigrette (below)

Combine the spinach, cranberries, almonds and apple in a large bowl. Add enough Honey Mustard Vinaigrette to coat and toss to mix gently.

Yield: 4 to 6 servings

Honey Mustard Vinaigrette

$1/2$ cup olive oil
2 tablespoons Dijon mustard
1 teaspoon dry mustard
$3/4$ cup cider vinegar
$1/4$ cup honey

Whisk the olive oil, Dijon mustard, dry mustard, vinegar and honey in a bowl until mixed.

NOTE: Any remaining vinaigrette can be stored, covered, in the refrigerator for up to 1 month.

Yield: about $1 1/2$ cups

Sweet Strawberry Salad

2 tablespoons butter, melted
$^1/_2$ cup pecan halves
16 ounces fresh spinach leaves, torn into bite-size pieces
1 pint strawberries, hulled, sliced
$^1/_2$ cup raspberry vinegar
$^1/_2$ cup olive oil
$^1/_2$ cup sugar
1 teaspoon salt
1 teaspoon dry mustard
$1^1/_2$ teaspoons poppy seeds

Pour the melted butter into a 9×9-inch baking pan and tilt to coat the bottom of the pan. Add the pecans and stir to coat. Bake at 350 degrees for 10 minutes or until pecans are lightly browned. Set aside and let the pecans cool completely.

Combine the spinach, strawberries and cooled pecans in a large bowl. Combine the vinegar, olive oil, sugar, salt and dry mustard in a jar with a tight-fitting lid. Shake until well mixed. Add to the spinach mixture and toss to mix. Sprinkle with the poppy seeds. Cover and chill for 30 minutes before serving.

NOTE: You may substitute raspberries for the strawberries.

Yield: 6 to 8 servings

Tropical Fruit Salad

1 cup pineapple juice
1/4 cup orange juice
3 tablespoons lemon juice
2/3 cup sugar
2 tablespoons flour
2 eggs, beaten
1 tablespoon butter
2 (16-ounce) cans crushed pineapple, drained
2 (16-ounce) cans fruit cocktail, drained
2 (15-ounce) cans mandarin oranges, drained
2 bananas, sliced
2 cups whipping cream, whipped

Combine the pineapple juice, orange juice, lemon juice, sugar, flour, eggs and butter in a saucepan. Bring to a boil over medium heat and boil for 1 minute, stirring constantly. Remove from the heat and let cool to room temperature.

Combine the pineapple, fruit cocktail and mandarin oranges in a bowl. Fold in the cooled juice mixture. Cover and chill thoroughly. Fold in the bananas. Fold in the whipped cream.

Yield: 6 to 8 servings

Citrus Iced Tea

2 cups water
6 tea bags
1/3 to 1/2 cup sugar
2 tablespoons each fresh
 orange juice and fresh
 lemon juice
2 cups ice water
Orange slices
Lemon slices

Bring 2 cups water to a boil in a saucepan. Remove from the heat and add the tea bags. Let steep for 15 to 20 minutes. Remove and discard the tea bags. Add the sugar and stir until the sugar dissolves. Let stand until cooled. Pour the tea into a pitcher. Stir in the orange juice, lemon juice and 2 cups ice water. Add orange and lemon slices and chill. Serve over ice. Garnish each glass with an additional orange or lemon slice and mint leaves.

Variation: You may use lemons only or oranges only for a different taste. A fruity herbal tea may be substituted for regular tea if desired.

Yield: 4 servings

Rice and Black-Eyed Pea Salad

2 (10-ounce) packages frozen black-eyed peas
Salt to taste
1 1/2 cups uncooked rice
1/4 cup cider vinegar
1 teaspoon cumin
1 teaspoon minced garlic
1 1/2 teaspoons salt
1 teaspoon pepper
1/3 cup olive oil
2 cups chopped celery
1 (10-ounce) package frozen corn kernels, thawed
1/2 cup chopped fresh cilantro
1/4 cup minced jalapeño chiles

Cook the black-eyed peas in boiling salted water in a saucepan for
20 minutes. Drain. Cook the rice according to the package directions.
Pour the rice into a sieve. Rinse with warm water and drain.

Whisk the vinegar, cumin, garlic, 1 1/2 teaspoons salt and pepper in a large
bowl. Whisk the olive oil in gradually. Add the warm peas and rice and toss
to coat. Add the celery, corn, cilantro and jalapeños. Toss to mix well.

Yield: 12 servings

Sweet-and-Sour Black-Eyed Peas

1/2 cup vegetable oil
3 tablespoons cider vinegar
1 tablespoon Dijon mustard
2 teaspoons sugar
1/2 teaspoon salt
1/2 teaspoon (or less) pepper
1 large Granny Smith apple, peeled, cored, cut into chunks
1 large red bell pepper, seeded, chopped
6 green onions, sliced
1/2 to 3/4 cup finely chopped cooked ham
1 (15-ounce) can black-eyed peas

Combine the vegetable oil, vinegar, Dijon mustard, sugar, salt, pepper and apple in a food processor container and pulse until the apple is coarsely chopped.

Combine the bell pepper, green onions, ham and black-eyed peas in a medium bowl and mix well. Add the apple mixture to the bell pepper mixture and stir to mix.

NOTE: This salad is great for a summer barbecue. It can also be served as a main dish or side dish.

Yield: 6 servings

Valley of Fire

Valley of Fire is Nevada's oldest and largest state park. The valley derives its name from the red sandstone formations and stark beauty of the Mojave Desert. Ancient remnants of early man can be found throughout the park in 3,000-year-old petroglyphs. The park is located 55 miles northeast of Las Vegas.

Sliced Tomatoes Vinaigrette

8 medium to large tomatoes, peeled
1/2 cup finely chopped fresh parsley
1/2 cup finely chopped celery
1/4 cup finely chopped onion
1 tablespoon sugar
1 teaspoon seasoned salt
1/2 teaspoon pepper
1/4 teaspoon each dried thyme and curry powder
1 cup olive oil or vegetable oil
1/3 cup red wine vinegar

Core the tomatoes and cut into 1/2-inch slices. Arrange the slices in layers in a large shallow bowl. Combine the parsley, celery, onion, sugar, salt, pepper, thyme, curry powder, olive oil and vinegar in a jar with a tight-fitting lid. Shake to mix well. Pour over the tomatoes. Cover and chill for 1 hour or longer.

NOTE: You can add seasonal vegetables to this salad for a pleasant variation.

Yield: 6 to 8 servings

French Bread Salad

1 loaf crusty French bread, cut into cubes
4 cucumbers, cut into cubes
4 tomatoes, cut into cubes
1/2 cup chopped fresh parsley
3 cups (or less) cubed Cheddar, Swiss or mozzarella cheese
1 cup each canola oil and balsamic vinegar
2 garlic cloves, minced
Salt and pepper to taste

Combine the bread, cucumbers, tomatoes, parsley and cheese in a large bowl. Whisk the canola oil, vinegar and garlic in a small bowl. Season with salt and pepper. Add the dressing to the bread mixture and toss to coat. Let stand for 5 minutes to 1 hour for the bread to soak up the dressing.

NOTE: Dry bread works best in this recipe.

Yield: 6 servings

Chicken and Spinach Pasta Salad

4 boneless chicken breasts, grilled, chopped
1 cup seedless grape halves
1 cup sugar snap peas, blanched, cooled
2 to 3 cups baby spinach leaves
3 ounces corkscrew pasta, cooked, drained
3 to 4 green onions, chopped
Lemon Dressing (at right)

Combine the chicken, grapes, peas, spinach, pasta and green onions in a large bowl and mix well. Cover and chill. Add the Lemon Dressing and toss to mix.

Yield: 8 to 10 servings

Chicken and Wild Rice Salad

2 cups water
2/3 cup uncooked wild rice
1 teaspoon (heaping) salt
3 large boneless chicken breasts, cooked, chopped
1 large unpeeled Granny Smith apple, cored, chopped
1/3 small red onion, minced
1/2 cup raisins or dried cranberries
1/2 cup chopped celery (optional)
1/2 cup pecan pieces, toasted
2 tablespoons balsamic vinegar
2 tablespoons (or more) olive oil
Salt and pepper to taste

Heat the water to boiling in a saucepan. Add the rice and 1 teaspoon salt and cook until tender. Drain and place the rice in a large bowl. Add the chicken, apple, onion, raisins, celery, pecans, vinegar and olive oil. Season with salt and pepper to taste. Toss to mix. Serve immediately with a glass of cold Chateau Ste. Michelle Cold Creek Riesling.

VARIATION: Try substituting Candied Pecans (page 86) for the toasted pecans.

Yield: 4 to 6 servings

Lemon Dressing

1/2 cup olive oil
1/4 cup sugar
3 tablespoons balsamic vinegar
1/2 teaspoon (or more) salt
1/2 teaspoon dried minced onion
2 teaspoons lemon juice
2 to 3 tablespoons chopped fresh parsley

Whisk the olive oil, sugar, vinegar, salt, dried onion, lemon juice and parsley in a bowl until mixed.

Yield: 1 cup

Won Ton Chicken Salad

1/4 cup each honey and soy sauce
1/2 cup chicken broth
2 tablespoons ketchup
1/4 teaspoon each ginger and garlic powder
4 chicken breasts
1 package won ton wrappers
Sesame oil or vegetable oil
4 green onions, chopped
1 (11-ounce) can mandarin oranges, drained
1 cucumber, sliced
1 bunch romaine lettuce, sliced
2 carrots, peeled, shredded
1 head red cabbage, shredded
2 tablespoons each sesame seeds and slivered almonds, toasted
Garlic Ginger Vinaigrette (below)

Combine the honey, soy sauce, chicken broth, ketchup, ginger and garlic powder in a shallow dish. Stir to mix. Add the chicken and turn to coat. Cover and marinate in the refrigerator for 2 to 3 hours. Remove the chicken and discard the marinade. Grill or broil the chicken until cooked through. Cut into bite-size pieces and place in a large bowl.

Cut the won ton wrappers into 1/2-inch strips and brush with sesame oil. Place on a baking sheet and bake at 375 degrees for 5 to 10 minutes or until golden brown. Remove to paper towels and let cool slightly. Add to the chicken. Add the next 8 ingredients. Toss to mix. Add the Garlic Ginger Vinaigrette and toss to coat.

Yield: 4 to 6 servings

Garlic Ginger Vinaigrette

1/4 cup each vinegar, sugar and soy sauce
1/2 cup vegetable oil
1/2 teaspoon minced garlic
1/4 teaspoon ginger

Process the vinegar, sugar, soy sauce, vegetable oil, garlic and ginger in a blender until mixed well. Cover and chill.

Yield: 1 1/4 cups

Saturday Salad

1/2 cup walnut pieces
8 ounces pancetta, sliced
3 tablespoons Dijon mustard
1 tablespoon chopped fresh tarragon, or 1 teaspoon
   dried tarragon
1 garlic clove, minced
2 tablespoons lemon juice
2 whole chicken breasts, skinned, boned
1 garlic clove, minced
3/4 cup Basic Vinaigrette (at right)
Salt and pepper to taste
6 medium Belgian endive, torn into bite-size pieces
4 ounces mushrooms, thinly sliced
1 large tomato, peeled, cut into bite-size pieces
2 tablespoons finely chopped fresh chives

Place the walnuts in a single layer on a baking sheet. Bake at 350 degrees for 7 to 10 minutes or until lightly browned. Remove to a plate to cool. Cook the pancetta in a skillet over medium-low heat until crisp and lightly browned. Remove to paper towels to drain.

Combine the Dijon mustard, tarragon, 1 garlic clove and lemon juice in a shallow bowl. Add the chicken and turn to coat. Cover and marinate in the refrigerator for 30 minutes or longer. Remove the chicken to a baking dish and cover with foil. Discard the remaining marinade. Bake at 350 degrees for 20 minutes or until cooked through. Remove the chicken to a cutting surface and cut into 2-inch pieces. Pour the pan juices into a small bowl. Whisk in 1 garlic clove and 3/4 cup Basic Vinaigrette. Season with salt and pepper.

Combine the walnuts, pancetta, chicken, endive, mushrooms, tomato and chives in a bowl. Add the Basic Vinaigrette mixture and toss to coat. Serve immediately.

Yield: 4 to 6 servings

Basic Vinaigrette

1/4 cup red wine vinegar
1 teaspoon Dijon mustard
1 shallot, finely chopped
1/2 cup vegetable oil
1/4 cup olive oil
1/2 teaspoon salt
1/8 teaspoon finely
   ground pepper

Whisk the vinegar, Dijon mustard and shallot in a bowl. Whisk in the vegetable oil and olive oil gradually. Continue whisking until well blended. Whisk in the salt and pepper.

Note: Any remaining vinaigrette can be stored, covered, in the refrigerator for up to 1 month.

Yield: 1 cup

Thai Chicken Salad

2 tablespoons peanut oil
1/4 cup soy sauce
1/4 cup honey
1 whole chicken breast, skinned, boned
1/2 cup corn oil
1/4 cup sesame oil
1 tablespoon red pepper flakes
1/4 cup soy sauce
6 tablespoons honey
2 teaspoons salt
1 pound linguini, tagliarini or oriental noodles
1/2 cup chopped roasted peanuts
2 tablespoons sesame seeds, toasted
1/2 cup chopped green onions
1/4 cup chopped fresh cilantro
1 large carrot, julienned
1/2 red bell pepper, julienned
4 ounces Chinese pea pods, blanched or slightly steamed

Combine the peanut oil, 1/4 cup soy sauce and 1/4 cup honey in a shallow bowl. Add the chicken and turn to coat. Cover and marinate in the refrigerator for about 1 hour. Remove the chicken to a baking dish and discard the marinade. Bake the chicken at 400 degrees for 30 minutes or until cooked through. Remove to a cutting surface. Cool and cut into bite-size pieces.

Combine the corn oil, sesame oil and red pepper flakes in a saucepan and heat over medium heat until hot and fragrant. Remove from the heat and stir in 1/4 cup soy sauce, 6 tablespoons honey and salt. Cook the linguini according to package directions. Drain and place in a large bowl. Add the hot dressing and toss to coat. Add the peanuts, sesame seeds, green onions, cilantro, carrot, bell pepper, pea pods and cooked chicken and toss to mix. Chill until serving time. Serve cold.

Yield: 4 to 6 servings

Chicken Salad Cassidy

This recipe was provided by David Cassidy.

2 tablespoons Dijon mustard
1/3 cup tamari
Splash of balsamic vinegar
2 whole chicken breasts, cut into small strips
1 teaspoon butter
1 teaspoon olive oil
Salt to taste
1 to 2 heads romaine lettuce
Assorted mixed greens
1 green onion, chopped
Raisins (optional)
Sunflower seed kernels (optional)
Sliced beets (optional)
1 hard-cooked egg, sliced (optional)
Equal parts of olive oil, Dijon mustard and tarragon vinegar
1/2 teaspoon (or less) salt

Mix the mustard, tamari and balsamic vinegar in a medium bowl. Add the chicken strips and stir to coat. Let marinate for 15 minutes. Melt the butter with 1 teaspoon olive oil in a skillet. Season with salt to taste. Heat until hot and add the chicken and marinade mixture. Cook until the chicken is browned and cooked through. Set aside and keep warm.

Combine the romaine lettuce, mixed greens, green onion, raisins and sunflower seeds. Top with sliced beets and sliced egg. Cover with the chicken and pan juices. Whisk the olive oil, mustard, tarragon vinegar and 1/2 teaspoon salt in a small bowl until creamy. Pour over the salad and toss to coat.

Yield: 2 to 4 servings

David Cassidy

David Cassidy is a visible force in Las Vegas, both in the showrooms and in the community. His high-energy performances have been witnessed by many in EFX at the MGM Grand and At the Copa at the Rio. He has also served as Grand Marshal in the Henderson Industrial Days Parade. He organized a celebrity charity golf tournament to give back to the community that he and his family call home–Las Vegas.

Sesame Shrimp Salad

2 tablespoons butter
2 (3-ounce) packages ramen noodles, crumbled
2/3 cup slivered almonds
1/2 cup sesame seeds
4 heads butter lettuce, torn into bite-size pieces
Sesame Dressing (below)
1 cup thinly sliced green onions
1 1/2 pounds small shrimp, cooked, peeled, deveined

Melt the butter in a 10-inch skillet over medium-high heat. Add the noodles
and almonds. Cook for 5 minutes or until lightly browned, stirring frequently.
Add the sesame seeds and cook for 1 minute or until toasted, stirring
constantly. Remove to paper towels to cool.

Combine the lettuce with 1 cup of the Sesame Dressing in a bowl. Toss to
coat. Divide the lettuce among 8 plates. Sprinkle with the toasted noodle
mixture and green onions. Top with the shrimp. Drizzle with the
remaining dressing.

Yield: 8 servings

Sesame Dressing

3/4 cup rice vinegar
1/3 cup vegetable oil
1/4 cup packed brown sugar
1 tablespoon soy sauce
1 tablespoon sesame oil

Combine the vinegar, vegetable oil, brown sugar, soy sauce and sesame
oil in a jar with a tight-fitting lid. Shake until mixed well.

Yield: about 1 1/3 cups

Soy Orange Vinaigrette

This recipe was provided by chef Steve Zucker.

2 cups frozen orange juice concentrate, thawed
3/4 cup soy sauce
3/4 cup balsamic vinegar
1 tablespoon pomegranate molasses or other molasses
1/4 cup corn syrup
4 cups olive oil
Salt and pepper to taste

Combine the orange juice concentrate, soy sauce, vinegar, molasses and corn syrup in a bowl and mix well. Add the olive oil gradually, whisking constantly until blended. Season with salt and pepper to taste. Serve over your favorite mixed greens.

Yield: about 8 cups

Steve Zucker

Chef Steve Zucker of Bix's Restaurant is passionate about food, and he creates some of the best cuisine in the valley. He and his talented crew bring diners a unique, modern American menu.

Champagne Brunch

Breads and Brunch

*pictured at left: Asparagus Tart
(recipe on page 77),
Orange Sour Cream Muffins
(page 73), and
Melon in Rum Lime Sauce
(page 196)*

Cranberry Orange Bread

2 cups flour
$1/2$ teaspoon salt
$1^1/2$ teaspoons baking powder
$1/2$ teaspoon baking soda
1 cup sugar
Grated peel of 1 orange
2 tablespoons vegetable oil
Juice of 1 orange
1 egg, beaten
1 cup chopped walnuts
1 cup coarsely chopped fresh cranberries

Sift the flour, salt, baking powder, baking soda and sugar into a bowl.
Add the grated orange peel. Pour the vegetable oil into a 1-cup measuring
cup. Add the orange juice. Add enough water to measure $3/4$ cup. Stir the
juice mixture lightly into the dry ingredients. Add the egg, walnuts and
cranberries and mix well. Spoon the batter into a greased and floured loaf
pan. Bake at 350 degrees for 1 hour or until a wooden pick inserted near
the center comes out clean. Remove to a wire rack to cool.

Yield: 10 to 12 servings

Feta Bread Roll

1 frozen uncooked pizza dough, thawed
Olive oil
1 (32-ounce) jar marinated artichoke hearts, drained, quartered
1 large jar roasted peppers
1 cup crumbled feta cheese

Roll the pizza dough into a thin layer on a floured surface. Brush with
olive oil. Layer the artichoke hearts, peppers and cheese in the center.
Fold the sides in and pinch together at the top. Brush with olive oil.
Place on a greased baking sheet. Bake at 450 degrees for 15 to
20 minutes or until golden brown.

VARIATION: Use pepperoni or various cheeses in the filling.

Yield: 10 to 12 servings

Hawaiian Nut Bread

3 cups flour
2 cups sugar
1 teaspoon baking soda
1 teaspoon salt
1 teaspoon cinnamon
1 cup chopped pecans or walnuts
3 eggs, beaten
1 (8-ounce) can crushed pineapple, drained
1$\frac{1}{2}$ cups vegetable oil
2 cups mashed bananas
2 teaspoons vanilla extract

Combine the flour, sugar, baking soda, salt and cinnamon in a medium bowl and mix well. Stir in the pecans. Combine the eggs, pineapple, vegetable oil, bananas and vanilla in a large bowl and mix well. Add the dry ingredients to the egg mixture and stir just until moistened.

Spoon the batter into 2 greased and floured loaf pans. Bake at 350 degrees for 1 hour and 5 minutes or until a wooden pick inserted near the center comes out clean. Remove to a wire rack to cool.

Yield: 20 to 24 servings

Holiday Coffee and Bears

Every Christmas a dedicated group of sustainer members conduct the Holiday Bear Project. League members and their guests adopt "bears"—each "bear" representing a needy child and the child's holiday wish list. Gifts including clothes, toys, and books are brought to the annual Holiday Coffee and then later delivered to the "bears." This thirty-plus-year project has grown to make Christmas brighter for more than 400 children in Las Vegas.

Croustades of Cheese and Dill

8 slices sourdough bread
Melted butter
1½ cups shredded Swiss cheese
6 tablespoons sour cream
3 tablespoons chopped fresh chives
½ teaspoon dried dill

Brush the bread with melted butter. Mix the cheese, sour cream, chives and dill in a bowl. Spread on the bread slices. Place on an ungreased baking sheet. Broil for 1 minute or until the cheese is bubbly. Serve hot with soup or salad.

Yield: 8 servings

Italian Corn Muffins

1½ cups flour
½ cup yellow cornmeal
2 tablespoons sugar
1 tablespoon baking powder
½ teaspoon salt
2 plum tomatoes, seeded, chopped
¼ cup chopped fresh oregano or basil
1 cup milk
¼ cup extra-virgin olive oil
1 egg, lightly beaten
12 (¾-inch) cubes mozzarella cheese

Combine the flour, cornmeal, sugar, baking powder and salt in a large bowl. Add the tomatoes and oregano and toss to mix. Mix the milk, olive oil and egg in a medium bowl. Add to the flour mixture, stirring just until moistened.

Spoon half the batter into nonstick muffin cups. Top each with 1 cheese cube. Cover with the remaining batter. Bake at 400 degrees for 20 to 25 minutes or until the muffins test done. Let stand for 5 minutes. Serve warm.

Yield: 1 dozen

Orange Sour Cream Muffins

These muffins are pictured on page 68.

6 tablespoons butter, softened
1 cup sugar
1 egg
1/2 cup sour cream
1/2 teaspoon orange extract
1 1/4 cups flour
1/2 teaspoon baking soda
1/2 teaspoon salt
1/2 cup chopped pecans
3 tablespoons grated orange peel
3 tablespoons orange juice

Combine the butter and sugar in a mixing bowl. Beat with an electric mixer until light and fluffy. Beat in the egg. Add the sour cream and orange extract and mix well. Sift the flour, baking soda and salt into a small bowl. Add the flour mixture to the sour cream mixture and mix well. Stir in the pecans, orange peel and orange juice.

Coat miniature muffin cups with nonstick cooking spray. Fill the muffin cups 3/4 full with batter. Bake at 375 degrees for 12 minutes or until a wooden pick inserted near the center comes out clean. Remove to a wire rack to cool.

Yield: 1 dozen

Garlic Cheese Bread

1 cup (2 sticks) butter, softened
1 tablespoon minced garlic
1 tablespoon paprika
1 tablespoon dried parsley flakes
1/2 cup grated Parmesan cheese
1/2 cup finely shredded Cheddar cheese
1 loaf Italian bread, cut into 1/2-inch slices

Combine the butter, garlic, paprika, parsley flakes, Parmesan cheese and Cheddar cheese in a bowl. Stir until mixed well. Spread the cheese mixture on the bread slices and place on an ungreased baking sheet. Bake at 425 degrees for 5 to 8 minutes or until golden brown. Serve hot.

Yield: 8 servings

Butterhorn Rolls

1 cake yeast
1 tablespoon warm (110-degree) water
1/8 teaspoon salt
1 cup warm (110-degree) milk
1/2 cup (scant) sugar
1/2 cup (1 stick) butter, melted, cooled
3 eggs, beaten
4 cups sifted flour
Melted butter

Dissolve the yeast in the warm water in a large bowl. Add the salt, warm milk, sugar, 1/2 cup melted butter and eggs and mix well. Add the flour gradually, stirring until a smooth dough forms. Cover and chill overnight.

Divide the dough into 3 or 4 equal portions. Roll each portion into a circle on a lightly floured surface. Brush with melted butter. Cut each circle into 12 wedges. Starting at the wide end, roll each wedge into a crescent. Place the rolls 2 inches apart on greased baking sheets. Cover with a damp towel and let rise in a warm place until doubled in bulk. Remove the towel. Bake at 350 degrees for 10 minutes or until golden brown.

NOTE: You may substitute 1 cup of whole wheat flour for 1 cup of the all-purpose flour.

Yield: 3 to 4 dozen

Blueberry Poppy Seed Brunch Cake

2/3 cup sugar
1/2 cup (1 stick) butter, softened
1 egg
2 teaspoons grated lemon peel
1 1/2 cups flour
2 tablespoons poppy seeds
1/2 teaspoon baking soda
1/4 teaspoon salt
1/2 cup sour cream
1/3 cup sugar
2 teaspoons flour
2 cups fresh blueberries or
    drained thawed frozen blueberries
1/4 teaspoon milk
1/3 cup confectioners' sugar
2 to 4 teaspoons milk

Beat 2/3 cup sugar and butter in a large bowl with an electric mixer until light and fluffy. Add the egg and lemon peel and beat at medium speed for 2 minutes. Mix 1 1/2 cups flour, poppy seeds, baking soda and salt in a bowl. Add to the butter mixture alternately with the sour cream, beating well after each addition. Spread the batter on the bottom and 1 inch up the side of a greased and floured 9- or 10-inch springform pan, making sure the batter is 1/4 inch thick at the side.

Mix 1/3 cup sugar and 2 teaspoons flour in a bowl. Add the blueberries and 1/4 teaspoon milk. Stir lightly to coat the blueberries without crushing. Spoon the blueberry mixture into the center of the batter. Bake at 350 degrees for 45 to 55 minutes or until the crust is golden brown. Place the pan on a wire rack and cool slightly. Loosen the coffee cake from the side of the pan with a sharp knife and remove the side of the pan. Combine the confectioners' sugar and 2 to 4 teaspoons milk in a small bowl. Stir until smooth. Drizzle over the warm coffee cake. Serve warm or at room temperature.

Yield: 8 servings

Champagne Brunch Menu

Sweet Strawberry Salad (page 56)

Blueberry Poppy Seed Brunch Cake (at left)

Tahoe Egg Bake (page 80)

Lemon Limeade (page 81)

Apple and Cheddar Quiche

2 medium cooking apples, peeled, cored, shredded
1/2 cup white port or sauterne
1 unbaked (10-inch) pie pastry
1 1/2 cups shredded Cheddar cheese
3 eggs
1 1/2 cups light cream
1/4 teaspoon nutmeg

Place the shredded apples in a bowl. Add the white port and stir to coat. Let marinate for 1 hour or longer. Drain and discard any liquid. Line a quiche dish or pie plate with the pie pastry. Sprinkle the marinated apples and cheese over the pastry. Beat the eggs, cream and nutmeg in a bowl. Pour over the apples and cheese. Bake at 375 degrees for 40 to 50 minutes or until a knife inserted near the center comes out clean. Let stand for 15 minutes before cutting. Garnish with apple slices and shredded Cheddar cheese.

NOTE: Rome Beauty or Granny Smith apples work well in this recipe.

Yield: 6 to 8 servings

Bacon Quiche

1 pound bacon, crisp-cooked
1 unbaked (9-inch) pie shell
1 cup shredded Swiss cheese or Cheddar cheese
4 eggs, beaten
Sugar to taste
1/8 teaspoon each nutmeg and cayenne pepper, or to taste
1/4 teaspoon salt
2 cups half-and-half

Crumble the bacon into the pie shell. Sprinkle the cheese over the bacon. Combine the remaining ingredients in a mixing bowl. Beat for 1 minute or longer. Pour into the pie shell. Bake on the lowest rack at 400 degrees for 15 minutes. Reduce the oven temperature to 325 degrees. Bake for 30 minutes or until a knife inserted near the center comes out clean. Serve hot or cold.

NOTE: You may substitute chopped cooked ham for the bacon.

Yield: 6 to 8 servings

Asparagus Tart

This tart is pictured on page 68.

1 teaspoon flour
1 unbaked (10-inch) pie pastry
14 ounces asparagus, cut into 3-inch spears
Salt to taste
2/3 cup half-and-half
2 eggs
1/2 cup grated Parmesan cheese
1 tablespoon chopped fresh tarragon, or
    1 teaspoon dried tarragon
1/2 teaspoon salt
Pepper to taste

Rub the flour over 1 side of the pie pastry. Arrange the pastry floured side down in a 9-inch tart pan. Press the dough into the pan. Fold the excess dough at the top over 2 times to form a thick edge. Prick the bottom and side with a fork. Bake at 450 degrees for 15 minutes or until golden brown. Cool on a wire rack.

Cook the asparagus in boiling salted water in a saucepan for 4 minutes or until tender-crisp. Drain and pat dry. Arrange the spears in spoke-fashion on the bottom of the baked crust, with the tips at the outside.

Beat the half-and-half, eggs, Parmesan cheese, tarragon, 1/2 teaspoon salt and pepper in a bowl. Pour over the asparagus. Bake at 375 degrees for 35 minutes or until puffed and golden brown. Place on a wire rack to cool slightly and set. Serve warm.

Yield: 4 servings

Fabulous Eggnog

12 eggs, separated
    (see Note)
1 1/3 cups sugar
4 cups milk
2 cups heavy cream
1/2 cup bourbon
1/2 cup brandy

Beat the egg whites in a bowl until stiff but not dry. Set aside. Combine the egg yolks and sugar in a bowl. Beat until thick and pale yellow. Stir in the milk, cream, bourbon and brandy slowly. Fold in the beaten egg whites. Serve in 7-ounce Fizz glasses. Garnish with a dusting of nutmeg.

Note: To avoid raw eggs that may carry salmonella, use an equivalent amount of pasteurized egg substitute.

Yield: 12 servings

Warm Fruit Compote

1 (12-ounce) package dried prunes
1 (11-ounce) package dried apricots
1 (15-ounce) can pear halves, drained
1 (15-ounce) can peach halves, drained
1 (15-ounce) can pitted cherries, drained
1 (15-ounce) can pineapple chunks, drained
2/3 cup currants
Grated peel and sections of 1 orange
Grated peel and sections of 1 lemon
1 cup packed brown sugar
1 cup macaroon cookie crumbs
1/2 cup tawny port

Combine the prunes, apricots, pears, peaches, cherries, pineapple, currants, orange peel, orange sections, lemon peel and lemon sections in a large bowl and mix well. Spoon into a greased large baking dish.

Combine the brown sugar and macaroon crumbs in a bowl and mix well. Sprinkle over the fruit. Bake at 325 degrees for 1 hour and 20 minutes. Remove from the oven and pour the port over the top. Return to the oven and bake for 15 minutes. Serve warm, cold or at room temperature.

NOTE: This is a wonderful side dish with turkey, pork or lamb. It is also good for a holiday buffet.

Yield: 12 to 15 servings

Blueberries Bryan

This recipe was provided by Senator Richard Bryan.

French bread, cut into 3/4-inch slices
8 eggs
1 cup milk
3/4 teaspoon vanilla extract
1/2 cup (1 stick) butter, softened
1 cup packed brown sugar
1/4 cup flour
1 cup rolled oats
1 cup chopped walnuts
1 to 2 cups fresh blueberries

Place the bread slices in a greased 6×10-inch baking dish. Cut extra bread to fill in any open spaces on the bottom. Beat the eggs in a bowl. Stir in the milk and vanilla. Pour over the bread slices. Let stand for 1 to 2 minutes for the bread to soak up the liquid. Turn the bread slices over to evenly soak the other side.

Combine the butter, brown sugar and flour in a bowl. Mix with a pastry blender. Stir in the oats. Sprinkle over the soaked bread. Top evenly with the walnuts and blueberries. Bake at 375 degrees for 30 to 40 minutes or until puffed and the edges are bubbling. Cool on a wire rack for 5 minutes. Cut into squares to serve.

Yield: 8 servings

Richard Bryan

Senator Richard Bryan is a native of southern Nevada, where his aptitude for leadership and public service revealed itself at an early age. In 1964, Bryan became a deputy district attorney in Las Vegas. Two years later, he was appointed Clark County's first public defender. His legislative service began in 1968, when he was elected to the Nevada State Assembly. Following a second term in the Assembly, he was elected to the Nevada State Senate in 1972 and again in 1976. In 1978, Bryan was elected Nevada Attorney General, serving in that capacity until 1982. In 1982, he was elected to the first of two terms as Nevada's governor. In 1988, Bryan ran for the United States Senate, where he currently serves. He and his wife, Bonnie, have devoted much time and energy to charitable organizations throughout Nevada.

Tahoe Egg Bake

1/2 cup (1 stick) butter
8 ounces mushrooms, sliced
2 cups thinly sliced yellow onions
Salt and pepper to taste
2 to 3 tablespoons butter, softened
12 slices white bread, crusts removed
1 1/2 pounds mild Italian sausage, cooked, cut into bite-size pieces
1 pound Cheddar cheese, shredded
5 eggs
2 1/2 cups milk
1 tablespoon Dijon mustard
1 teaspoon each dry mustard, nutmeg and salt
1/4 teaspoon pepper
2 tablespoons finely chopped fresh parsley

Melt 1/2 cup butter in a 12-inch skillet. Add the mushrooms and onions and sauté over medium heat for 5 to 8 minutes or until tender. Season with salt and pepper to taste. Butter the bread slices with 2 to 3 tablespoons butter.

Layer the bread, mushroom mixture, sausage and cheese 1/2 at a time in a greased 7×11-inch baking dish. Beat the eggs, milk, Dijon mustard, dry mustard, nutmeg, 1 teaspoon salt and 1/4 teaspoon pepper in a medium bowl. Pour over the sausage mixture. Cover and chill overnight.

Sprinkle the parsley evenly over the top of the casserole. Bake at 350 degrees for 1 hour or until bubbly. Serve immediately.

VARIATION: For a milder version, substitute 1 1/2 cups chopped green onions for the yellow onions and 1 pound Monterey Jack cheese for the Cheddar cheese. For a Mexican version, substitute chorizo for the Italian sausage and cilantro for the parsley.

Yield: 8 servings

Southwestern Strata

1 (16-ounce) package frozen corn kernels, thawed, drained
12 eggs, lightly beaten
12 ounces nonfat cottage cheese
2 cups shredded Monterey Jack cheese
1/2 cup (or more) salsa
1 (7-ounce) can chopped green chiles, drained
1/2 cup flour
1 teaspoon baking soda

Spread the corn in a greased 9×11-inch baking dish. Mix the next 5 ingredients in a bowl. Add a mixture of the flour and baking soda to the egg mixture; mix well. Pour over the corn. Place the baking dish in a larger baking pan. Add water to the larger pan to a depth of 1 inch. Bake at 350 degrees for 1 hour or until a knife inserted near the center comes out clean.

Yield: 10 servings

Traditional Holiday Punch

6 cups water
3 1/2 cups sugar
8 very ripe bananas
1 (46-ounce) can pineapple juice
1 (6-ounce) can frozen orange juice concentrate
1 (12-ounce) can frozen lemonade concentrate
8 liters lemon-lime soda

Combine the water and sugar in a 4-quart saucepan. Bring to a boil and boil for 5 minutes. Remove from the heat and let cool for 15 minutes. Purée the bananas in a food processor or blender. Mix the puréed bananas, sugar water, pineapple juice, orange juice concentrate and lemonade concentrate in a large container. Divide the mixture between 2 freezer containers. Freeze until solid. Remove from the freezer about 2 hours before serving. Add 4 liters lemon-lime soda to each container of frozen base. Break up the frozen base with a potato masher until slushy.

Yield: 50 servings

Lemon Limeade

1/2 cup sugar
1/2 cup water
1/4 cup fresh lime juice
1/4 cup fresh lemon juice
4 cups cold water

Combine the sugar and 1/2 cup water in a small saucepan. Simmer over low heat for 5 minutes, stirring constantly. Remove from the heat; let cool. Pour into a pitcher. Stir in the lime juice, lemon juice and 4 cups cold water. Chill thoroughly. Serve in tall tumblers filled with ice. Garnish with a lime or lemon slice and mint leaves.

Note: You may substitute carbonated or seltzer water for the 4 cups cold water.

Yield: 6 servings

Lounge Acts

Vegetables and Side Dishes

*pictured at left: Fresh Tomato
Risotto (recipe on page 92)*

Marinated Asparagus

1¹/₂ pounds asparagus
³/₄ cup olive oil
¹/₂ cup white wine vinegar
¹/₂ cup balsamic vinegar
¹/₄ cup sugar
1 tablespoon dried oregano
1 teaspoon salt
¹/₂ teaspoon pepper

Snap off the tough ends of the asparagus. Blanch or steam the asparagus until tender-crisp. Rinse under cold running water. Drain well and place in a shallow dish. Whisk the olive oil, white wine vinegar, balsamic vinegar, sugar, oregano, salt and pepper in a bowl. Pour over the asparagus. Cover and chill for several hours. Remove the asparagus from the marinade to serve.

Yield: 4 to 6 servings

Green Beans with Mustard Vinaigrette

2 pounds fresh green beans, ends trimmed
Salt to taste
2 shallots, minced
2 tablespoons Dijon mustard
2 tablespoons balsamic vinegar
¹/₂ cup olive oil
Freshly ground pepper to taste
¹/₄ cup chopped fresh dill

Cook the beans in boiling salted water in a saucepan until tender-crisp. Drain well and keep warm. Combine the shallots, Dijon mustard, vinegar, olive oil, salt and pepper in a small saucepan. Cook until heated through, whisking constantly. Toss the beans with the hot vinaigrette in a bowl. Add the dill and toss to combine. Serve immediately.

Yield: 6 to 8 servings

Nevada Barbecued Beans

1 pound pinto beans
10 cups cold water
$1/2$ teaspoon salt
8 ounces bacon, chopped
1 medium onion, chopped
1 rib celery, chopped
1 garlic clove, minced
$1/2$ cup tomato paste
$1/4$ cup chili sauce
2 tablespoons sugar
1 tablespoon dry mustard
1 tablespoon vinegar
1 teaspoon salt
$1/2$ teaspoon pepper

Sort and rinse the beans. Combine the beans and cold water in a Dutch oven. Let soak overnight. Add $1/2$ teaspoon salt to the soaking beans and bring to a simmer. Cover and simmer for $11/2$ to 2 hours or until tender. Drain the beans, reserving $31/2$ cups of the cooking liquid. Return the beans and reserved liquid to the Dutch oven and set aside.

Cook the bacon in a skillet until lightly browned. Drain off most of the drippings. Add the onion, celery and garlic to the skillet. Sauté for 10 minutes or until tender. Add the tomato paste, chili sauce, sugar, dry mustard, vinegar, 1 teaspoon salt and pepper. Bring to a boil, stirring constantly. Add the vegetable mixture to the beans and stir to mix. Bring to a simmer and cook, uncovered, for 45 minutes, stirring occasionally.

Yield: 6 to 8 servings

Nevada . . . Trick or Treat

The Treaty of Guadalupe Hidalgo, which concluded the Mexican War in 1848, granted the United States territory that included present-day Nevada. Statehood was granted on October 31, 1864, when President Abraham Lincoln secured the one vote needed for ratification of the Thirteenth Amendment abolishing slavery. Nevada, Spanish for "snow-capped," is often referred to as having been "Battle Born," and its nickname, the Silver State, was derived from its Civil War statehood and from the Union forces' use of Nevada gold and silver bullion to obtain credit throughout the war.

Pecan Carrots

2 tablespoons butter
2 teaspoons sugar
3 tablespoons water
Salt and pepper to taste
1 pound carrots, peeled, thinly sliced
Candied Pecans (below)

Melt the butter in a skillet. Stir in the sugar, water, salt and pepper. Add the carrots. Cover and cook over medium heat for 5 minutes. Uncover and cook for 3 minutes or until the carrots are tender-crisp. Stir in the Candied Pecans.

Yield: 6 servings

Candied Pecans

$1/2$ cup pecan halves
1 tablespoon butter
2 tablespoons light corn syrup
1 tablespoon sugar
$1/4$ teaspoon cinnamon
$1/8$ teaspoon salt, or to taste

Spread the pecans in a baking dish. Bake at 250 degrees until the pecans are hot. Melt the butter in a small saucepan. Stir in the corn syrup, sugar, cinnamon and salt. Simmer for 5 minutes. Pour the syrup over the pecans and stir to coat. Bake at 250 degrees for 1 hour, stirring every 20 minutes. Remove the pecans to another dish and let cool slightly. Separate the pecans with a fork and allow to cool completely.

NOTE: The pecans can be prepared up to a day ahead and stored in an airtight container.

Yield: $1/2$ cup

Carrot Soufflé

2 cups puréed cooked carrots
2 teaspoons lemon juice
2 tablespoons minced green onions
1/2 cup (1 stick) butter, softened
1/4 cup sugar
1 tablespoon flour
1 teaspoon salt
1/4 teaspoon cinnamon
1 cup milk
3 eggs, beaten

Combine the carrots, lemon juice, green onions, butter, sugar, flour, salt, cinnamon, milk and eggs in a bowl. Beat until smooth. Pour into a buttered 2-quart soufflé dish or casserole dish. Bake at 350 degrees for 45 to 60 minutes or until the center is set.

Yield: 4 to 6 servings

Baked Parsnips and Kumquats

1 pound parsnips, peeled, cut diagonally into
   1/4-inch strips
2 pears, peeled, sliced
12 kumquats, seeded, sliced crosswise
1/4 cup (1/2 stick) unsalted butter, melted
3 tablespoons brown sugar
3 tablespoons fresh orange juice
1 tablespoon orange liqueur

Arrange the parsnips and pears in alternating rows in a 10-inch oval or square au gratin dish. Insert the kumquat slices evenly throughout the rows. Mix the butter, brown sugar, orange juice and orange liqueur in a small bowl. Pour the mixture evenly over the fruit mixture. Cover the dish with foil and bake at 350 degrees for 45 minutes. Remove the foil and bake for 15 minutes or until the top is golden brown. Garnish with kumquat leaves for a touch of winter green.

Yield: 6 servings

Garlic Cream Cheese Mashed Potatoes

This dish is pictured on page 108.

2 pounds unpeeled new potatoes, cut into 1-inch cubes
1 teaspoon salt
1/2 cup (1 stick) butter, cut into pieces
4 ounces cream cheese, cut into pieces
5 (or more) garlic cloves, minced
1/2 cup finely chopped fresh parsley
1/4 cup grated Parmesan or Romano cheese
3/4 teaspoon salt
1/4 to 1/2 teaspoon white pepper
2 ounces Monterey Jack cheese, shredded

Place the potatoes in a saucepan. Add 1 teaspoon salt and enough water to cover the potatoes by 3 inches. Bring to a boil and boil until tender. Drain and place in a large bowl. Mash by hand for home-style potatoes or use an electric mixer for smoother potatoes.

Add the butter, cream cheese, garlic, parsley, Parmesan cheese, 3/4 teaspoon salt and white pepper to the potatoes and mix well. Spoon the potatoes into a greased 12-inch baking dish. Top with the Monterey Jack cheese. Bake at 450 degrees for 10 minutes or until the top is lightly browned.

VARIATION: Use minced chives or green onions in place of the parsley. Add 1/4 cup sautéed onion.

Yield: 10 to 12 servings

Crispy Baked Potatoes

    4 medium russet potatoes, cut into large wedges
    1 tablespoon vegetable oil
    1 tablespoon seasoned salt
    1/4 teaspoon freshly ground pepper
    1/8 teaspoon salt
    2 garlic cloves, minced

Place the potatoes in a bowl. Add the vegetable oil, seasoned salt, pepper and salt. Toss to coat the potatoes. Arrange the wedges in a single layer on a greased baking sheet. Bake at 425 degrees for 20 minutes. Turn the potatoes over and sprinkle with the garlic. Bake for 30 minutes or until golden brown.

NOTE: You may use your favorite seasonings to change the flavor.

    Yield: 4 servings

Gruyère Potato Gratin

    2 pounds large red potatoes
    Salt to taste
    1 1/2 cups shredded Gruyère cheese
    Pepper to taste
    2 eggs
    2 cups milk, heated just to boiling

Peel the potatoes and cut into 1/8-inch slices. Cook in boiling salted water in a saucepan for 4 minutes; drain well. Arrange 1/3 of the potatoes in a single layer in a buttered 1 1/2-quart au gratin dish or baking dish, overlapping the slices slightly. Top with 1/2 cup of the cheese and season with salt and pepper. Repeat the layers once. Top with the remaining potatoes. Whisk the eggs in a small bowl. Whisk in the hot milk slowly and season with salt and pepper. Pour the milk mixture evenly over the potatoes and top with the remaining 1/2 cup cheese. Bake at 400 degrees for 45 to 50 minutes or until the top is golden brown and the potatoes are tender.

    Yield: 4 to 6 servings

Dinner on the Patio Menu

Red Pepper Jelly (page 17)

Marinated Asparagus (page 84)

Crispy Baked Potatoes (at left)

Barbecued Leg of Lamb (page 110)

Grilled Fruit (page 194)

Stuffed Yellow Squash

4 medium yellow squash
3 slices bacon
4 green onions, chopped
1 teaspoon grated green bell pepper
3/4 cup fine dry bread crumbs
1/2 teaspoon pepper
1/4 teaspoon salt
3 tablespoons butter, melted
2 tablespoons plus 2 teaspoons grated Parmesan cheese

Place the squash in a large saucepan. Cover with water and bring to a boil. Cover the pan and reduce the heat. Simmer for 10 minutes or until the squash are tender but still firm. Drain and cool slightly. Trim off the stems and cut into halves lengthwise. Remove and reserve the pulp. Set the squash shells aside.

Fry the bacon in a skillet until crisp. Drain on paper towels and crumble when cool. Drain off the bacon drippings, leaving 1 1/2 teaspoons in the skillet. Add the green onions and bell pepper. Sauté until tender. Combine the reserved squash pulp, bacon, green onion mixture, bread crumbs, pepper, salt and butter in a bowl. Stir until mixed.

Spoon the squash mixture into the squash shells. Place in a 9×13-inch baking pan. Sprinkle the stuffed squash with the Parmesan cheese. Broil 4 inches from the heat source for 3 minutes or until lightly browned. Serve immediately.

Yield: 4 servings

Walnut Raisin Risotto

1/3 cup golden raisins
1 cup white wine
2 tablespoons butter
2 shallots, chopped
1/2 cup chopped walnuts
2 garlic cloves, minced
1 teaspoon allspice
1/8 teaspoon nutmeg, or to taste
2 cups arborio rice
Juice of 1 orange
3 cups hot vegetable stock
1 to 2 large heads Belgian endive, sliced
1 tablespoon chopped fresh oregano
1 cup grated Parmesan cheese

Place the raisins in a bowl and add the wine. Let soak for 30 minutes. Melt the butter in a heavy saucepan. Add the shallots, walnuts, garlic, allspice and nutmeg. Sauté for 4 minutes or until the shallots are tender.

Add the rice and cook over medium heat for 2 minutes, stirring constantly. Add the raisins, half the soaking liquid and orange juice. Cook until the liquid is absorbed, stirring constantly. Add the remaining soaking liquid and cook until the liquid is absorbed, stirring constantly. Add 3/4 cup of the hot vegetable stock and cook until the stock is absorbed, stirring constantly. Add 1 1/2 cups of the stock 3/4 cup at a time, cooking until the stock is absorbed before adding more and stirring constantly. When 3/4 cup of the stock is remaining, add half of it and cook until absorbed, stirring constantly. Test the rice; it should be tender but firm. Add the remaining stock if needed. The total cooking time should be about 20 minutes.

Stir in the endive and cook for 2 to 3 minutes. Stir in the oregano and Parmesan cheese. Garnish with grated orange peel and chopped fresh oregano.

VARIATION: Use dried cranberries in place of raisins and cranberry juice for the orange juice. Substitute almonds or pecans for the walnuts.

Yield: 4 to 6 servings

Hoover Dam

Located 30 miles southeast of Las Vegas, Hoover Dam is clearly visible from the air when descending into McCarran International Airport. The dam is 727 feet high, 1,244 feet long, 660 feet thick at the base, and 45 feet thick at the crest. It weighs 5,500,000 tons and contains 3,250,000 cubic yards of concrete, enough for a 16-foot-wide highway that could extend from San Francisco to New York City. The project took four years to complete and supplies electrical power for three states. The dam truly is an engineering wonder of the modern world. Its price tag of $48,890,955 was a fortune during the Depression of the 1930s.

Spanish Rice

6 to 8 slices bacon, cut into 1/2-inch pieces
1 medium onion, chopped
1/3 cup chopped green bell pepper
1 (10-ounce) can tomato soup
2 cups cooked white rice
1/4 cup shredded Cheddar cheese

Fry the bacon in a skillet until crisp. Remove the bacon and drain on paper towels. Add the onion and bell pepper to the bacon drippings. Sauté until translucent but not browned. Remove the onion and bell pepper to a bowl. Add the bacon, tomato soup and rice to the bowl. Add some of the bacon drippings for flavor if desired. Stir to combine. Spoon into a 1 1/2-quart baking dish. Sprinkle with the cheese. Bake at 350 degrees for 30 minutes or until bubbly.

NOTE: This dish can be made up to 1 day ahead and baked just before serving.

Yield: 8 to 10 servings

Toasted Rice

1 cup uncooked rice
2 tablespoons butter
2 cups beef broth
3 green onions, thinly sliced
1 tablespoon soy sauce

Spread the rice in a heavy baking pan. Bake at 350 degrees for 10 to 15 minutes or until toasted a golden brown color. Melt the butter in a heavy 2-quart saucepan. Stir in the toasted rice. Add the beef broth and bring to a boil. Cover and reduce the heat. Simmer for 25 minutes. Remove from the heat and stir in the green onions and soy sauce. Cover and let stand for a few minutes for the flavors to blend.

NOTE: This is delicious with chicken, pork or lamb.

Yield: 4 servings

Mediterranean Poultry Stuffing

1 cup pine nuts
2 tablespoons olive oil
1½ pounds ground lamb or ground beef
3 cups uncooked white rice
6 cups chicken broth
2 teaspoons salt
½ teaspoon pepper
¾ teaspoon ground allspice

Combine the pine nuts and olive oil in a large stockpot. Sauté until the pine nuts are golden brown. Crumble the lamb into the stockpot. Stir in the rice, chicken broth, salt, pepper and allspice. Bring to a boil and reduce the heat to low. Simmer for 20 minutes or until the rice is cooked and the liquid is absorbed. Let cool before stuffing poultry.

Yield: about 14 cups

Drunken Cranberries

1 pound fresh cranberries
⅓ cup brandy
2 cups sugar

Combine the cranberries, brandy and sugar in a large bowl and mix well. Spoon into a 1½-quart baking dish. Bake, covered, at 350 degrees for 1 hour.

NOTE: This dish is a wonderful accompaniment to pork or turkey.

Yield: 8 servings

Headliners

Entrées

pictured at left: Cornish Game Hen with Amaretto Stuffing (recipe on page 137)

Steak with Wild Mushroom Cream Sauce

1 tablespoon olive oil
1 shallot, minced
1/2 cup brandy
2 cups beef stock
1/2 cup heavy cream
8 ounces fresh wild mushrooms (such as chanterelle, morel or oyster)
    or button mushrooms, sliced
Salt and pepper to taste
1 tablespoon butter
1 tablespoon olive oil
2 (8-ounce) sirloin steaks, 3/4 inch thick

Heat 1 tablespoon olive oil in a heavy skillet over medium heat. Add the
shallot and sauté for 3 minutes. Remove the skillet from the heat. Add the
brandy and ignite it with a match. Return the skillet to the heat when the
flames subside. Add the beef stock. Boil for 15 minutes or until reduced to
about 1/2 cup, stirring occasionally. Add the cream and bring to a boil. Stir
in the mushrooms and reduce the heat. Simmer for 20 minutes or until the
mushrooms are tender, stirring occasionally. Season with salt and pepper.

Melt the butter with 1 tablespoon olive oil in a heavy skillet over high heat.
Add the steaks. Cook for 2 minutes or until brown on both sides. Reduce
the heat. Cook for 3 minutes per side for medium-rare. Remove steaks to
serving plates and keep warm. Add the mushroom sauce to the skillet
and simmer, scraping up browned bits. Spoon the sauce over the steaks.
Serve with Ruffino Aziano.

Yield: 2 servings

Peppered Filet Mignon

This recipe was provided by chef Henry Garcia.

1/2 teaspoon whole coriander, coarsely ground
1 teaspoon coarsely ground pepper
1 (8-ounce) beef tenderloin
1 teaspoon butter
1/4 teaspoon minced garlic
1/4 teaspoon minced shallots
1/4 cup brandy
1/3 cup heavy cream
Salt to taste

Mix the coriander and pepper in a shallow bowl. Cut the tenderloin into medallions and coat with the pepper mixture. Melt the butter in a skillet over medium-high heat. Add the beef medallions and cook until golden brown. Add the garlic and shallots and sauté for 2 minutes.

Remove the skillet from the heat. Add the brandy and ignite it with a match. Return the skillet to the heat when the flames subside. Add the cream and simmer until slightly thickened. Season with salt.

Yield: 2 servings

Henry Garcia

Henry Garcia is the Executive Chef at Sunset Station.

Steak Diane

1 (1½-pound) beef tenderloin, trimmed
1 to 1½ tablespoons coarsely ground pepper
1 tablespoon butter
¾ cup finely chopped shallots
¼ cup dry white wine
¼ cup white wine vinegar
½ cup beef broth
2 teaspoons dry mustard
1 tablespoon Dijon mustard
½ cup heavy cream
Salt to taste
1 tablespoon butter
2 tablespoons dry sherry
2 tablespoons brandy

Cut the tenderloin into 1½-inch-wide steaks. Lay each steak on its cut side and press to flatten. Sprinkle both sides of the steaks with pepper and press the pepper onto the surface. Melt 1 tablespoon butter in a 12-inch nonstick skillet over high heat. Add the shallots and sauté for 1½ minutes or until shallots are soft. Add the wine, vinegar, broth, dry mustard, Dijon mustard and cream. Season with salt. Bring to a boil over high heat. Cook until reduced by ½, stirring constantly. Pour the sauce into a small bowl and set aside.

Clean and dry the skillet. Return the skillet to high heat. Add 1 tablespoon butter and swirl until the butter melts. Add the steaks, making sure not to overlap. Cook for 2 minutes or until browned. Turn the steaks over and cook 2 minutes longer for rare. Remove the beef to a warm plate and cover to keep warm. Add the sherry and brandy to the skillet and heat to boiling. Stir in the cream sauce and any juices drained from the cooked steaks. Cook until heated through. Spoon the sauce onto individual serving plates and top with the steaks.

Yield: 6 servings

Salt-Encrusted Beef Tenderloin

2 cups kosher salt
1/4 cup fresh thyme leaves
1 tablespoon minced fresh rosemary
2 egg whites
2/3 cup water
2 to 3 cups flour
1 tablespoon unsalted butter
1 tablespoon olive oil
1 (2-pound) beef tenderloin, about 4 inches long and
    4 inches thick
1 teaspoon fresh thyme leaves
Freshly ground pepper to taste
1 egg yolk
1/2 teaspoon water
2 tablespoons coarse sea salt

Combine the kosher salt, 1/4 cup thyme, rosemary, egg whites, 2/3 cup water and 2 cups of the flour in a bowl and mix well. Mix by hand to form a dough. Add enough additional flour so that the dough is firm and not moist or sticky. Melt the butter with the olive oil in a skillet. Add the tenderloin and brown for 2 to 3 minutes per side. Remove to an inverted salad plate.

Roll the dough out on a lightly floured work surface, making certain it is large enough to enclose the tenderloin. Place the tenderloin in the center of the dough. Sprinkle with 1 teaspoon thyme and season with pepper. Wrap the dough around the tenderloin and press all seams to seal. Mix the egg yolk with 1/2 teaspoon water in a small bowl and brush over the dough. Sprinkle with the coarse salt. Place on a baking sheet. Bake at 375 degrees for 30 minutes. Remove from the oven and let stand at room temperature for 1 to 1 1/2 hours. Remove the crust and discard. Cut the beef into slices to serve.

NOTE: This tenderloin always comes out medium to medium-rare and delicious.

Yield: 6 to 8 servings

Spicy Beef Marinade

3 garlic cloves, minced
3 tablespoons balsamic vinegar
1/4 cup soy sauce
2 tablespoons Worcestershire sauce
2 teaspoons dry mustard
1 cup beef broth
1/4 cup merlot or cabernet sauvignon (optional)
Freshly ground pepper

Combine the garlic, vinegar, soy sauce, Worcestershire sauce, dry mustard, broth and wine in a shallow dish. Rub the beef you plan to marinate with ground pepper. Add to the marinade, turning to coat. Cover and chill for 6 to 12 hours. Remove the beef and discard the marinade. Grill or roast to desired degree of doneness. Use for London broil, kabobs, roasts and fillets.

Yield: 1 3/4 cups

Spinach Meat Loaf

1 pound ground beef or ground turkey
1 egg
Salt and pepper to taste
1 (10-ounce) package frozen chopped spinach, thawed, drained
1/2 to 3/4 cup grated Parmesan cheese
1/2 to 3/4 cup shredded mozzarella cheese
3 to 4 cups marinara sauce

Mix the ground beef and egg in a bowl. Season with salt and pepper. Pat into a rectangle. Mix the spinach, Parmesan cheese and mozzarella cheese in a bowl. Spread on top of the ground beef. Roll up, starting at the short side. Pinch the ends so that no spinach shows. Place in a loaf pan. Bake at 375 degrees for 45 minutes. Cover the top with marinara sauce. Bake for 30 minutes longer. Top with additional mozzarella cheese during the last 5 minutes baking time if desired.

Yield: 6 to 8 servings

Mayoral Meatballs

This recipe was provided by Mayor Oscar Goodman.

2 pounds ground beef or ground turkey
2 eggs, beaten
1/2 cup bread crumbs
1 to 2 garlic cloves, minced
1/2 cup chopped fresh parsley
1/2 cup grated Romano cheese
1/2 teaspoon salt
1/4 teaspoon coarsely ground pepper
Garlic powder to taste
1 tablespoon olive oil or vegetable oil

Combine the ground beef, eggs, bread crumbs, garlic, parsley, cheese, salt and pepper in a bowl and mix well. Season with garlic powder. Shape into 1-inch balls. Heat the olive oil in a large skillet. Add the meatballs and brown on all sides. Reduce the heat and cook until the meatballs are cooked through. Remove to paper towels to drain.

NOTE: This mixture also makes a great meat loaf. Shape into a loaf and place in a loaf pan. Bake at 350 degrees for 1 to 1 1/2 hours. Use a combination of ground beef and ground turkey if desired.

Yield: 48 meatballs

Oscar Goodman

Mayor Oscar Goodman was born in Philadelphia and graduated from the University of Pennsylvania Law School. He moved to Las Vegas in 1964 and soon became one of the city's premier criminal defense attorneys. Goodman has been recognized for his distinguished legal career by being named one of the "Fifteen Best Trial Lawyers in America" by the National Law Journal *and is listed annually in the "Best Lawyers in America." His wife, Carolyn, is the founder and president of the Meadows School, the only nonprofit and nonsectarian private school in Nevada.*

Strudel Beef Roll

2 tablespoons butter
1 small onion, chopped
8 ounces mushrooms, chopped
2 pounds lean ground beef
1 1/2 teaspoons salt
1/4 teaspoon pepper
1/2 teaspoon dried oregano
2 garlic cloves, minced
3 eggs
1 1/2 cups shredded Swiss cheese
1/4 cup finely chopped parsley
1/4 cup fine dry bread crumbs
12 sheets phyllo dough (see Note)
2 tablespoons butter, melted

Melt 2 tablespoons butter in a skillet. Add the onion and sauté until translucent. Add the mushrooms and ground beef and sauté until the ground beef is brown. Remove to a bowl. Stir in the salt, pepper, oregano and garlic. Let cool slightly. Add the eggs and mix lightly. Stir in the cheese, parsley and bread crumbs. Cover and chill.

Place 6 sheets of phyllo dough on a work surface, overlapping them to make a 15×24-inch rectangle and brushing each sheet with some of the 2 tablespoons melted butter. Spread half the filling over the phyllo to within 1 1/2 inches of the long side and 3 inches from the end. Fold the 1 1/2-inch edge over the filling. Fold the 3-inch edge over the filling. Roll as for a jelly roll. Repeat with remaining phyllo dough and filling. Place the rolls in a 10×15-inch baking pan. Brush with melted butter. Bake at 325 degrees for 30 to 35 minutes or until golden brown. Remove to a wire rack to cool slightly. Cut into 1 1/4-inch slices. Garnish with a dollop of sour cream. Serve hot.

NOTE: See pages 198 and 199 for directions on working with the phyllo dough.

Yield: 12 servings

Osso Buco

3 tablespoons butter
1 tablespoon olive oil
3 pounds veal shanks, cut 2 inches thick
1/2 cup flour
2 teaspoons salt
1/2 teaspoon pepper
1 medium onion, chopped
1/2 cup chopped carrot
1 teaspoon minced garlic
1/4 teaspoon dried marjoram
1/4 teaspoon dried thyme
1 teaspoon grated lemon peel
1 teaspoon grated orange peel
1 cup dry white wine
1 cup crushed tomatoes
2 cups (or more) chicken stock
1 bay leaf
1 tablespoon butter
1/2 cup cognac
1/2 cup finely chopped parsley

Melt 3 tablespoons butter with the olive oil in a large heavy saucepan. Coat the veal shanks in flour and add to the saucepan. Brown on all sides. Stir in the salt, pepper, onion, carrot, garlic, marjoram, thyme, lemon peel and orange peel. Cook over very low heat for 10 minutes or until the vegetables are tender. Add the wine and cook until almost evaporated. Stir in the tomatoes and chicken stock.

Cover the saucepan and cook over low heat for 1 1/2 hours or until the veal is tender. Add more chicken stock if the liquid evaporates too quickly. Add the bay leaf. Stir in 1 tablespoon butter and the cognac. Sprinkle with the parsley. Remove and discard the bay leaf. Serve over noodles or rice.

Yield: 6 servings

Veal with Spinach and Mustard Sauce

6 veal scaloppine (1½ pounds total)
1 cup half-and-half
3 tablespoons Creole mustard
2 tablespoons sour cream
½ cup flour
2 teaspoons Creole seasoning
6 tablespoons olive oil
1½ teaspoons butter
1½ teaspoons olive oil
1 teaspoon sesame seeds
2 teaspoons Creole seasoning
½ cup low-sodium chicken broth
1½ pounds fresh spinach, stems removed, cooked, drained, or
    2 (10-ounce) packages frozen leaf spinach, thawed, squeezed dry

Pound the scaloppine ¼ inch thick with a meat mallet. Set aside. Combine the half-and-half, mustard and sour cream in a small saucepan. Cook over low heat until heated through, whisking constantly. Set aside and keep warm.

Mix the flour and 2 teaspoons Creole seasoning in a shallow dish. Coat the veal with the flour mixture. Heat 2 tablespoons olive oil in a skillet over medium-high heat until hot. Add 2 scaloppine to the skillet. Cook for 1 minute or until firm. Remove to a platter and cover loosely with foil. Keep in a warm oven.

Continue with the remaining olive oil and veal. Drain the skillet when all the veal is cooked. Add the butter, 1½ teaspoons olive oil and sesame seeds. Cook for 2 minutes or until the sesame seeds are lightly browned, stirring constantly. Stir in 2 teaspoons Creole seasoning. Cook for 2 minutes, stirring constantly. Add the chicken broth and spinach. Cook for 5 minutes or until almost dry, stirring constantly. Ladle ¼ cup of warm mustard sauce onto each dinner plate. Spoon the spinach mixture onto the sauce and top with the veal.

NOTE: The key to this recipe is having everything ready before you start cooking.

Yield: 6 servings

French Veal Stew

2 pounds boneless veal, cut into bite-size pieces
2 whole black peppercorns
2 small garlic cloves, minced
3 sprigs of fresh parsley
1/4 teaspoon dried thyme
1 bay leaf
1 medium onion, finely chopped
1/2 cup dry white wine
2 cups beef broth
10 (about 1 1/2-inch diameter) small whole onions, peeled
1 cup heavy cream
Salt to taste

Combine the veal, peppercorns, garlic, parsley, thyme, bay leaf and chopped onion in a 4-quart Dutch oven. Cover and cook over medium heat for 30 minutes, stirring occasionally. Do not brown the veal. Stir in the wine and beef broth. Cover and simmer over low heat for 30 minutes. Add the small whole onions and simmer for 30 minutes or until the veal is very tender. Remove the veal and whole onions and set aside. Remove and discard the parsley and bay leaf.

Add the cream to the Dutch oven and bring to a boil. Boil rapidly for 8 to 10 minutes or until the sauce thickens. Return the veal, whole onions and any juices to the Dutch oven and heat through. Season with salt. Serve over rice.

NOTE: This dish can be made up to 2 days ahead. Cover and store in the refrigerator. Add a small amount of beef broth when reheating if needed.

Yield: 6 servings

Pickled Onions

4 medium red onions
1/2 cup water
1/2 cup sugar
1/2 cup white vinegar

Peel the onions, leaving part of the root end to help hold their shape during cooking. Cut each onion into quarters and place in a saucepan. Add the water, sugar and white vinegar. Bring to a boil, stirring occasionally. Reduce the heat and simmer for 7 minutes or until tender-crisp. Spoon onions and liquid into an airtight container. Store in the refrigerator. These onions make a nice garnish and are especially good with beef and pork.

Yield: 8 servings

Rack of Lamb with Mint Stuffing

1 (7-ounce) package herb-seasoned cubed stuffing mix
1 pound ground lamb
1/4 cup finely chopped onion
1 tart apple, peeled, cored, finely chopped
1 teaspoon fresh lemon juice
1 tablespoon fresh or dried mint leaves, finely chopped
1 tablespoon water
1/4 teaspoon paprika
1/4 teaspoon pepper
1 teaspoon salt
1 (5- to 6-pound) crown roast of lamb
Salt and pepper to taste
1 tablespoon dried mint leaves
1 tablespoon vinegar
1/2 cup red currant jelly
1 tablespoon grated orange peel
2 tablespoons finely chopped fresh mint leaves

Prepare the stuffing mix using the package directions. Brown the ground lamb with the onion in a skillet, stirring frequently. Add the apple, lemon juice, 1 tablespoon mint, water, paprika, pepper and 1 teaspoon salt. Remove from the heat. Stir in the prepared stuffing. Set aside and keep warm.

Season the roast with salt and pepper. Wrap the bone ends in foil. Place on a rack in a roasting pan. Bake at 325 degrees for 30 minutes per pound. Remove from the oven 45 minutes before the roast is done. Fill the center with some of the stuffing. Cover the top of the roast with foil. Place the remaining stuffing in a 1 1/2-quart casserole. Place the roasting pan and the casserole in the oven. Bake for 45 minutes.

Mix 1 tablespoon mint and vinegar in a bowl. Let stand for 2 minutes; drain well. Discard the vinegar. Break the jelly into pieces with a fork. Stir in the orange peel, 2 tablespoons mint and vinegar-soaked mint.

Remove the roast from the oven. Let stand for 10 minutes. Cover bone ends with paper frills. Serve the sauce and additional stuffing on the side.

Yield: 6 to 8 servings

Barbecued Leg of Lamb

1 boned leg of lamb
8 to 9 garlic cloves
1 cup honey
2/3 cup dried mint flakes
1 bottle chenin blanc

Remove the membrane from the lamb with a sharp small knife. Make 8 or 9 slits in the lamb. Insert 1 garlic clove in each slit. Coat the lamb with the honey and sprinkle with the mint. Press the mint onto the surface of the lamb. Place in a sealable plastic bag. Add the wine and seal the bag. Marinate in the refrigerator for 1 to 3 days, turning occasionally. Remove the lamb and discard the marinade. Grill over hot coals for 45 minutes or until cooked through.

Yield: 6 to 8 servings

Pork Tenderloin with Rosemary

2 (12-ounce) pork tenderloins
1/2 teaspoon salt
1/8 teaspoon pepper, or to taste
1/2 cup bread crumbs
1/2 teaspoon crumbled dried rosemary
1 egg, lightly beaten
2 tablespoons vegetable oil
1 cup chopped celery
1/2 cup water

Season the pork with the salt and pepper. Mix the bread crumbs and rosemary in a shallow dish. Dip the tenderloins in the egg and then in the bread crumb mixture. Heat the vegetable oil in a skillet. Add the breaded tenderloins and brown on all sides. Stir in the celery and water. Reduce the heat and cover the skillet. Simmer over low heat for 30 minutes. Uncover for the last 5 minutes of cooking to crisp the coating. Cut into slices to serve.

Yield: 4 to 6 servings

Blackened Pork Loin

This recipe was provided by chef William Pfersching.

Minced garlic to taste
Granulated garlic to taste
Paprika to taste
Chili powder to taste
Cayenne pepper to taste
Salt and black pepper to taste
1 or 2 pork tenderloins
Watermelon and Papaya Salsa (below)

Mix the minced garlic, granulated garlic, paprika, chili powder, cayenne pepper, salt and black pepper in a bowl (prepare enough to generously coat the tenderloin). Spread the seasoning mixture over the pork. Grill on all sides to brown. Place in a roasting pan and bake at 325 degrees until cooked through. Slice the pork and spread in a fan shape on a serving platter. Cover with some of the Watermelon and Papaya Salsa. Serve the remaining salsa on the side.

Yield: 3 to 6 servings

William Pfersching

William Pfersching is the Executive Chef at Canyon Gate Country Club in Las Vegas.

Watermelon and Papaya Salsa

1/2 medium seedless watermelon
4 ripe papaya
3/4 (4-inch-diameter) jicama
2 jalapeño chiles, seeded, minced
1/2 bunch cilantro, finely chopped
Juice of 4 limes
1/2 cup sherry wine vinegar
1/2 teaspoon cayenne pepper
Salt and black pepper to taste

Cut the watermelon, papaya and jicama into small cubes. Combine with the jalapeños and cilantro in a bowl and mix gently. Stir in the lime juice, vinegar and cayenne pepper. Season with salt and black pepper. Stir to mix well.

NOTE: This recipe may be halved.

Yield: 20 servings

Barbecued Pork Tenderloin

1 1/2 teaspoons salt
1 to 2 tablespoons sugar
2 garlic cloves, minced
5 tablespoons soy sauce
3 tablespoons applesauce
2 tablespoons sherry
2 pork tenderloins

Mix the salt, sugar, garlic, soy sauce, applesauce and sherry in a bowl. Add the tenderloins, turning to coat. Cover and chill for 3 hours or longer. Remove the tenderloins to a 9×11-inch roasting pan. Add half the marinade to the pan; discard the remaining marinade. Bake at 375 degrees for 45 to 60 minutes or until cooked through.

Yield: 4 to 6 servings

Penne Puttanesca

3 cups chopped seeded peeled fresh tomatoes
1/2 cup olive oil
2 tablespoons minced garlic
1 tablespoon minced shallots
3 tablespoons drained capers
1/2 cup chopped green olives
1/4 cup chopped fresh basil
1 teaspoon crushed red pepper
6 anchovy fillets, finely chopped (optional)
16 ounces penne
Grated Parmesan cheese to taste

Place the chopped tomatoes in a colander and drain to remove excess liquid. Heat the olive oil in a saucepan. Add the garlic and shallots and sauté until tender but not browned. Stir in the drained tomatoes, capers, olives, basil, red pepper and anchovies. Simmer for 15 minutes. Cook the pasta in boiling salted water in a stockpot until al dente. Drain and place in a large bowl. Add the tomato sauce and toss to coat. Sprinkle with Parmesan cheese and toss to mix.

Yield: 4 servings

Macaroni "Magic"

This recipe was provided by Lance Burton. The "magic" macaroni disappears in your mouth.

4 ounces uncooked elbow macaroni
Salt to taste
1 tablespoon butter or margarine
1/4 cup chopped onion
1 tablespoon flour
1/8 teaspoon pepper, or to taste
1 1/4 cups milk
2 cups shredded American, Swiss or sharp Cheddar cheese
1 medium tomato, sliced (optional)

Cook the macaroni in boiling salted water in a stockpot until al dente; drain well. Melt the butter in a saucepan. Add the onion and sauté until tender but not brown. Stir in the flour and pepper. Add the milk and cheese all at once. Cook until the cheese is melted, stirring constantly. Add the cooked macaroni and mix well.

Spoon into a 2-quart baking dish. Bake at 350 degrees for 25 to 30 minutes or until bubbly. Arrange the tomato slices on top during the last 5 minutes of cooking time. Remove from the oven and let stand for 10 minutes before serving.

Yield: 4 servings

Lance Burton

During the 1980s and 1990s, Lance Burton rose to become the number one prestidigitator in the international community of magicians. In July of 1980, he became the first person to win magic's most coveted Gold Medal Award for Excellence from the International Brotherhood of Magicians. In July 1982, Burton was the recipient of magic's highest accolade when he won the Grand Prix at the Federation International Society de Magic (F.I.S.M.) in Lausanne, Switzerland, making him a world-champion magician. He achieved a dream come true when he opened the Lance Burton Theatre at the Monte Carlo Resort and Casino in Las Vegas.

Four-Cheese Pasta

2³/4 pounds tomatoes, cored, seeded, chopped
¹/2 cup chopped fresh basil
1¹/2 teaspoons coarsely chopped garlic
1 large garlic clove, minced
1 cup ricotta cheese
2 tablespoons (or more) heavy cream
Salt and freshly ground pepper to taste
Freshly ground nutmeg to taste
2 ounces fontina cheese, cut into ¹/4-inch cubes
2 ounces fresh mozzarella cheese, cut into ¹/4-inch cubes
1 pound uncooked pasta
2 tablespoons olive oil
1 cup grated Parmesan cheese

Combine the tomatoes, basil and garlic in a bowl and mix well. Let stand for 1 to 2 hours, stirring occasionally. Fluff the ricotta cheese with a fork in a bowl. Stir in enough cream to make of a creamy consistency. Season with salt, pepper and nutmeg. Stir in the fontina cheese and mozzarella cheese.

Cook the pasta in boiling salted water in a stockpot until al dente. Drain well. Toss the hot pasta and olive oil in a bowl. Add the cheese mixture and toss to coat well. Add the Parmesan cheese and toss to mix well. Drain most of the liquid from the tomato mixture, leaving just enough to keep the mixture moist. Spoon the hot pasta onto serving plates and top with the tomato mixture.

Yield: 4 to 6 servings

Roasted Red Pepper Rigatoni

1 red bell pepper, halved, seeded
1 tablespoon olive oil
1/2 cup chopped onion
1 garlic clove, minced
1 (14-ounce) can diced peeled tomatoes
1/8 teaspoon salt
1/8 teaspoon white pepper
8 ounces rigatoni, cooked al dente
1 tablespoon olive oil
1/4 cup grated Parmesan cheese
2 tablespoons fresh basil, sliced into ribbons (see Note)

Place the bell pepper halves skin side up on a broiler pan and press down to flatten. Broil for 10 minutes or until the skin is blackened. Remove the pepper to a small paper or sealable plastic bag. Seal and let stand for 5 to 10 minutes. Remove from the bag and rub off the blackened skin with your fingers. Cut the pepper halves into 1/2-inch pieces.

Heat 1 tablespoon olive oil in a skillet over medium heat. Add the onion and garlic and sauté for 3 minutes. Add the undrained tomatoes, salt and white pepper. Simmer until most of the liquid evaporates. Stir in the roasted bell pepper and cook until heated through. Toss the pasta and 1 tablespoon olive oil in a bowl. Add the tomato mixture and Parmesan cheese and toss to coat. Top with the basil ribbons. Serve warm.

NOTE: Make basil ribbons by rolling a basil leaf lengthwise. Cut into thin slices; when unrolled, you will have thin strands of basil.

Yield: 4 servings

Mount Charleston

The mountains located at the west of the Las Vegas Valley are part of the 316,000 acres that make up the Spring Mountain Recreation Area. The mountains contain a variety of plant and animal species not found anywhere else. Inside the national forest, the topography changes from desert into Joshua and yucca forests and then to juniper, aspen, ponderosa, and bristlecone forests. Recreation includes hiking, camping, picnicking, and skiing. Mount Charleston is located 35 miles northwest of Las Vegas.

Vermicelli au Gratin

3 tablespoons vegetable oil
8 ounces Mexican vermicelli or Italian-style vermicelli (see Note)
1 onion, finely chopped
1 garlic clove, minced
1 pound fresh tomatoes, peeled, chopped, partially drained, or
    1 (35-ounce) can plum tomatoes, drained, chopped
1/2 teaspoon dried oregano
1 1/2 cups beef stock or beef broth
Salt and pepper to taste
1/2 cup freshly grated Parmesan cheese

Heat the vegetable oil in a cast-iron skillet over medium-high heat. Sauté the vermicelli in batches for 15 to 30 seconds or until golden brown. Remove to paper towels to drain. Add the onion, garlic and tomatoes to the skillet. Sauté over medium heat for 5 minutes. Stir in the oregano and beef stock. Season with salt and pepper.

Place the vermicelli in a Dutch oven and add the tomato mixture. Cover and simmer for 15 minutes or until the liquid is absorbed. Uncover and sprinkle with the Parmesan cheese. Broil 4 inches from the heat source for 30 seconds or until the cheese melts.

NOTE: Mexican vermicelli can be found at Hispanic markets. Leave Mexican vermicelli whole; break Italian-style vermicelli into 2-inch pieces.

Yield: 6 servings

Sweet Sausage Bowties

Vegetable oil
1 pound sweet Italian sausage, casings removed, crumbled
1/2 teaspoon crushed red pepper
1/2 cup finely chopped onion
3 garlic cloves, minced
2 cups chopped seeded peeled Roma tomatoes, or
    1 (28-ounce) can tomatoes, drained, coarsely chopped
1 1/2 cups heavy cream
1/2 teaspoon salt
2 teaspoons pesto (optional)
Freshly ground black pepper to taste
12 ounces uncooked farfalle (bowties)
Salt to taste
3 tablespoons finely chopped fresh parsley
3/4 to 1 cup grated Parmesan cheese

Heat a small amount of vegetable oil in a heavy skillet over medium heat. Add the sausage and red pepper. Sauté for 7 minutes or until the sausage is no longer pink. Add the onion and garlic and sauté until the onion is tender and the sausage is lightly browned. Stir in the tomatoes, cream, 1/2 teaspoon salt and pesto. Season with black pepper. Simmer for 4 minutes or until the mixture is slightly thickened and the flavors have blended.

Cook the pasta in boiling salted water in a stockpot until al dente. Drain and add to the sausage mixture in the skillet. Cook for 2 minutes, stirring occasionally. Add the parsley and Parmesan cheese. Toss to mix well.

Yield: 6 to 8 servings

Polo Pasta

1 pound smoked turkey sausage
1/4 cup olive oil
2 tablespoons minced onion
2 garlic cloves, minced
8 ounces fresh mushrooms, sliced
2 (14-ounce) cans stewed Italian tomatoes
12 ounces spinach fettuccini, cooked al dente
Grated Parmesan cheese to taste

Cut the sausage diagonally into 1/4-inch slices. Heat the olive oil in a saucepan over medium heat. Add the sausage, onion and garlic and sauté for 5 minutes. Add the mushrooms and sauté until the mushrooms are slightly wilted. Stir in the tomatoes, breaking any large pieces into bite-size pieces. Simmer until the liquid is reduced by 1/3. Divide the fettuccini among individual serving plates. Top with the mushroom sauce. Sprinkle with Parmesan cheese.

Yield: 6 to 8 servings

Smoked Salmon Linguini

1 tablespoon each butter and olive oil
2 to 3 garlic cloves, minced
8 ounces sliced smoked salmon, cut into thin strips
1/2 cup pesto
1/4 cup white wine
1 (15-ounce) can peeled tomatoes, drained
1/2 cup evaporated milk
Salt and pepper to taste
8 ounces uncooked linguini
2 tablespoons chopped fresh parsley

Melt the butter with the olive oil in a saucepan. Add the garlic and sauté until golden brown. Add the salmon and sauté gently for 1 minute. Stir in the pesto, wine and tomatoes. Simmer for 5 minutes. Stir in the evaporated milk and simmer for 3 minutes. Season with salt and pepper. Cook the linguini in boiling salted water in a stockpot until al dente. Drain and return to the stockpot. Stir in a small amount of the sauce. Remove the linguini to a serving bowl. Pour the remaining sauce over the top and sprinkle with the parsley.

Yield: 4 servings

Shrimp and Asparagus Pasta

1 pound asparagus spears, trimmed, cut into halves
2 large shallots, minced
1/2 cup chicken broth
2 teaspoons chopped fresh thyme
1/2 teaspoon crushed red pepper flakes
1/4 teaspoon salt
1 pound uncooked medium shrimp, peeled, deveined
1/2 cup heavy cream
1 tablespoon butter
2 tablespoons lemon juice
8 ounces uncooked pasta
Salt to taste

Combine the asparagus, shallots, chicken broth, thyme, red pepper and 1/4 teaspoon salt in a large skillet and mix well. Bring to a boil. Reduce the heat and simmer until the asparagus is tender. Remove the asparagus to a plate with a slotted spoon and keep warm. Add the shrimp to the skillet and cook for 2 to 3 minutes or until opaque. Remove the shrimp with a slotted spoon and add to the asparagus. Add the cream to the skillet and bring to a boil. Cook for 2 to 3 minutes, stirring constantly. Remove from the heat. Stir in the butter and lemon juice.

Cook the pasta in boiling salted water in a stockpot until al dente; drain well. Place the pasta in a serving bowl. Return the skillet to the heat. Add the shrimp and asparagus and cook until heated through. Pour over the pasta and toss to mix well.

Yield: 6 servings

Fettuccini with Bay Scallops and Shrimp

2 tablespoons butter
1 tablespoon olive oil
1/2 cup chopped shallots
8 ounces uncooked medium shrimp, peeled, deveined
8 ounces bay scallops
1 teaspoon chopped fresh basil
1 tablespoon chopped fresh dill
3/4 cup white wine
1 cup half-and-half
1 pound uncooked spinach fettuccini
Salt to taste
2 tablespoons butter
1/2 cup grated Parmesan cheese

Melt 2 tablespoons butter with the olive oil in a large skillet. Add the shallots and sauté for 2 to 3 minutes or until tender but not browned. Add the shrimp and scallops and sauté for 1 minute. Stir in the basil, dill and wine. Reduce the heat and simmer until the mixture is reduced by 1/2. Add the half-and-half and cook until the mixture thickens, stirring constantly. Remove from the heat and keep warm.

Cook the fettuccini in boiling salted water in a stockpot until al dente. Drain and toss with 2 tablespoons butter and the Parmesan cheese in a serving bowl. Add the seafood mixture and toss to mix. Serve with warm sourdough bread.

Yield: 4 to 6 servings

Porcini Sauce

2 ounces dried porcini mushrooms
Hot chicken broth or water
3 tablespoons butter
2 tablespoons chopped shallots
2 tablespoons flour
1/2 garlic clove, minced
1 cup heavy cream
1/2 cup chicken broth
1 tablespoon butter
1/2 teaspoon dried thyme
Chopped fresh parsley to taste
Salt and pepper to taste

Place the dried mushrooms in a bowl. Cover with hot chicken broth.
Let soak for 20 to 30 minutes. Remove the mushrooms and squeeze dry.
Reserve the soaking liquid. Rinse the mushrooms and pat dry. Chop and
set aside.

Melt 3 tablespoons butter in a saucepan. Add the shallots and sauté until
tender but not browned. Stir in the flour. Add the garlic, cream and 1/2 cup
chicken broth. Cook until thickened, stirring constantly. Remove from
the heat.

Melt 1 tablespoon butter in a skillet. Add the chopped mushrooms and
sauté until heated through. Stir in the thyme. Season with parsley, salt and
pepper. Add the cream mixture to the skillet. Add mushroom liquid to
taste. Cook until thick, stirring constantly. Serve over fettuccini or other
favorite cooked pasta.

NOTE: Be careful when adding the mushroom liquid—too much will
overpower the other flavors in the sauce.

Yield: about 2 cups

Summer Pasta Sauce

2 pounds ripe tomatoes, peeled, cored, chopped
1/4 cup chopped fresh parsley
1/4 cup chopped fresh basil
2 garlic cloves, minced
1/4 cup olive oil
1/8 teaspoon crushed red pepper, or to taste
Salt to taste

Mix the tomatoes, parsley, basil, garlic, olive oil, red pepper and salt in a large glass bowl. Cover and chill for 1 hour or longer. Toss the chilled sauce with cooled cooked linguini or other pasta. Top each serving with finely grated Parmesan or asiago cheese if desired.

Yield: 6 servings

Basil Pesto

2 cups packed fresh basil
1/4 cup pine nuts, lightly toasted
2 garlic cloves
1/2 cup freshly grated Parmesan cheese
2 tablespoons freshly grated pecorino Romano cheese
Salt to taste
1/2 cup olive oil

Combine the basil, pine nuts, garlic, Parmesan cheese and Romano cheese in a food processor container. Season with salt. Process until all ingredients are finely chopped. Add the olive oil in a fine stream, processing constantly until well mixed. Use immediately or store in the refrigerator for up to 1 week. Cover the pesto with a thin layer of olive oil before refrigerating to prevent darkening.

Yield: about 1 1/2 cups

Fresh Basil Marinara with Chardonnay

8 ounces fresh basil leaves with stems
1/2 cup olive oil
2 cups finely chopped onions
10 garlic cloves, minced
1 (106-ounce) can crushed tomatoes
1 (106-ounce) can diced tomatoes
1 (6-ounce) can tomato paste
2 cups chardonnay
4 large carrots, peeled, cut into halves
3 1/2 teaspoons salt
3/4 teaspoon black pepper
1 teaspoon crushed red pepper
1 teaspoon each dried basil, oregano and Italian seasoning
1 garlic clove, minced

Remove the stems from the basil and place the stems on a square of cheesecloth. Divide the basil leaves in half. Chop half the basil and set aside. Chop the other half and add to the stems. Tie the basil and stems in the cheesecloth with a cotton string.

Heat the olive oil in an 8-quart stockpot over medium heat. Stir in the onions and cover the pan. Cook until the onions are translucent. Do not brown. Remove the cover and add 10 cloves minced garlic. Sauté for 1 minute or until slightly soft but not browned. Stir in the crushed tomatoes, diced tomatoes, tomato paste, chardonnay, carrots, basil stems in cheesecloth, salt, black pepper, red pepper, dried basil, oregano and Italian seasoning. Simmer over low heat for 3 1/2 hours, stirring occasionally. Stir in the reserved chopped basil and cook for 30 minutes. Cook longer if a thicker sauce is desired. Remove the basil in cheesecloth and the carrots and discard. Stir in 1 minced garlic clove. Cook for 5 minutes. Serve over pasta for a crowd or freeze for later use. Serve with Sebastiani Sonoma County Chardonnay.

NOTE: To reduce the amount of sauce by half, use two 28-ounce cans crushed tomatoes, two 28-ounce cans diced tomatoes and 3 ounces tomato paste. Reduce the salt to 1 1/2 teaspoons and reduce the remaining ingredients by half.

VARIATION: Try using a cabernet sauvignon or merlot in place of the chardonnay for a different flavor.

Yield: 30 servings

Peach Barbecue Sauce

This recipe was provided by chef Sheila Conway.

2$\frac{1}{2}$ medium peaches, peeled, pitted, chopped
$\frac{1}{2}$ cup sugar
$\frac{1}{3}$ cup packed brown sugar
1 tablespoon vanilla extract
1 teaspoon almond extract
$\frac{1}{2}$ cup (1 stick) butter
$\frac{1}{2}$ red onion, finely chopped
2 tablespoons minced garlic
1 cup red wine vinegar
$\frac{1}{2}$ cup soy sauce
$\frac{2}{3}$ cup Dijon mustard
$\frac{1}{2}$ cup packed brown sugar

Combine the peaches, sugar, $\frac{1}{3}$ cup brown sugar, vanilla and almond extract in a saucepan and mix well. Bring to a boil and reduce the heat. Simmer for 1 hour, mashing the peaches occasionally while cooking. Cook and mash until a preserve-like texture is achieved. Set aside.

Melt the butter in a heavy saucepan. Add the onion and garlic. Sauté until softened and just beginning to brown. Stir in the vinegar, soy sauce, Dijon mustard and $\frac{1}{2}$ cup brown sugar. Bring to a boil. Reduce the heat and stir in the peach mixture. Simmer until the volume is reduced by $\frac{1}{3}$ and the mixture has a shiny barbecue sauce texture. Mash the peaches occasionally while cooking. Use on salmon, chicken or pork. Store in the refrigerator.

Yield: about 4 cups

Sheila Conway

In January 2000, Canyon Gate Country Club's Executive Chef Sheila Conway won the People's Choice Award at the Chefs Des Chefs food show's cooking competition at Alexis Park. She won the competition with her recipe for peach barbecue center cut Frenched pork chops with roasted shallot whipped potatoes.

Chicken Angelo

3 whole skinless chicken breasts, boned
1 cup flour
1/4 cup clarified butter (see page 199)
1/8 teaspoon dried oregano, or to taste
Salt and pepper to taste
1/3 cup dry white wine
1 to 2 tablespoons fresh lemon juice
2 garlic cloves, minced
1/2 cup chicken broth
1 cup sliced mushrooms
6 canned or thawed frozen artichoke hearts, cut into quarters
1 tablespoon chopped fresh parsley

Cut the chicken into quarters. Coat with the flour, shaking off any excess. Heat the butter in a skillet over medium heat until hot. Add the chicken and brown on all sides. Add the oregano, salt and pepper.

Stir in the wine, lemon juice, garlic, chicken broth, mushrooms, artichoke hearts and parsley. Cook over high heat until the sauce thickens, stirring constantly. Serve immediately with rice and fresh vegetables.

Yield: 6 servings

Bleu Cheese-Encrusted Chicken

This recipe was provided by Rosie O'Donnell.

1/2 cup balsamic vinegar
1/4 cup olive oil
4 boneless skinless chicken breasts
1/4 cup olive oil
2 to 3 garlic cloves, minced
3/4 cup chopped sun-dried tomatoes
2 tablespoons capers
1/4 cup chopped green onions
3 ounces bleu cheese, crumbled

Mix the vinegar and 1/4 cup olive oil in a bowl. Add the chicken and turn to coat. Marinate, covered, in the refrigerator for 2 to 4 hours. Remove the chicken and reserve the marinade. Heat half of the remaining 1/4 cup olive oil in a skillet. Add the chicken and brown on all sides. Cook until the chicken is cooked through, adding small amounts of the reserved marinade while cooking. Remove the chicken to a baking dish.

Heat the remaining 2 tablespoons olive oil in a skillet. Add the garlic, tomatoes, capers and green onions. Sauté until the vegetables are very tender. Spoon the mixture on top of the chicken. Sprinkle evenly with the bleu cheese. Broil until the cheese is lightly browned.

Yield: 4 servings

Rosie O'Donnell

Rosie O'Donnell, five-time winner of the Star Search competition, has done stand-up comedy and broadcast her television show in Las Vegas show-rooms. She is known for her voluntarism and charitable contributions to breast cancer research and children's charities throughout the United States.

Chicken Piccata

6 boneless skinless chicken breasts
3 tablespoons Dijon mustard
2 eggs
1 cup seasoned bread crumbs
3 tablespoons olive oil
$1/2$ cup chicken broth
$1/4$ cup white wine
2 tablespoons lemon juice
2 tablespoons capers, drained
1 teaspoon salt
$1/2$ teaspoon white pepper
6 very thin lemon slices
1 tablespoon chopped fresh parsley

Pound the chicken breasts very thin. Whisk the Dijon mustard and eggs in a pie plate. Place the bread crumbs in another pie plate. Dip the chicken into the mustard mixture and then into the bread crumbs. Heat the olive oil in a very large skillet. Add the chicken and cook for 3 minutes per side or until browned and cooked through. Remove the chicken to a baking dish and keep warm in a 325-degree oven.

Add the chicken broth, wine, lemon juice, capers, salt and pepper to the skillet. Bring to a boil, scraping up browned bits. Reduce the heat and stir in the lemon slices and parsley. Cook for 10 minutes or until the lemon peel is soft. Place the chicken on serving plates and top with the sauce. Serve with Saint George STG Chalk Hill Chardonnay.

Yield: 6 servings

Breast of Chicken with Almonds

2 whole chicken breasts
Salt to taste
1 cup flour
1 egg, lightly beaten
1/4 cup finely chopped almonds
3 tablespoons butter
2 tablespoons sherry
1/2 teaspoon paprika
1 cup heavy cream
Lemon juice to taste (optional)
Chopped fresh parsley to taste (optional)
Chopped fresh basil to taste (optional)
Sautéed mushrooms to taste (optional)
Toasted chopped almonds (optional)

Season the chicken with salt. Coat with the flour. Dip the chicken in the beaten egg and then in the finely chopped almonds. Melt the butter in a skillet. Add the chicken and cook for 25 minutes or until golden brown and cooked through. Turn the chicken carefully while cooking to keep the almond coating intact. Remove the chicken to a baking dish and place in a warm oven.

Add the sherry, paprika and cream to the skillet. Simmer for 5 to 10 minutes, stirring occasionally. Stir in the lemon juice, parsley, basil and mushrooms. Cook until heated through, stirring in additional flour if needed to thicken the sauce. Cook until of the desired consistency. Place the chicken on serving plates. Top with the sauce and garnish with toasted chopped almonds.

Yield: 3 to 4 servings

Jezebel Sauce

1 (16-ounce) jar
  pineapple jelly
1 (8-ounce) jar pineapple
  preserves
1 (5-ounce) jar prepared
  horseradish
1 (2-ounce) can dry
  mustard
Salt and pepper to taste

Mix the pineapple jelly, pineapple preserves, horseradish and mustard in a bowl. Season with salt and pepper. Spoon into small jelly jars and cover tightly. Store in the refrigerator for up to 3 months. Serve over chicken, ham or other meats.

Note: Apricot jelly and preserves can be substituted for pineapple.

Yield: 6 (4-ounce) jars

Southwestern Grilled Chicken

2 tablespoons olive oil
1 garlic clove, minced
1 teaspoon chili powder
1 teaspoon ground cumin
1 teaspoon dried oregano
1/2 teaspoon salt
1 pound boneless skinless chicken breasts

Combine the olive oil, garlic, chili powder, cumin, oregano and salt in a small bowl and mix well. Brush the mixture on both sides of the chicken pieces to coat. Grill over medium heat for 8 to 10 minutes or until the chicken is cooked through. Serve with chopped cilantro, shredded lettuce, shredded cheese and chopped black olives.

Yield: 4 servings

Lemon Grilled Chicken

3/4 cup (1 1/2 sticks) butter
1/2 cup fresh lemon juice
1/3 cup water
1 teaspoon paprika
1/8 teaspoon cayenne pepper
2 tablespoons soy sauce
1 teaspoon honey
1 teaspoon Dijon mustard
2 garlic cloves, minced
1/2 teaspoon salt
2 broiler-fryers, quartered, or mixed chicken pieces

Combine the butter, lemon juice, water, paprika, cayenne pepper, soy sauce, honey, Dijon mustard, garlic and salt in a saucepan. Heat until the butter is melted, stirring constantly. Place the chicken on an oiled grill 5 to 6 inches above the coals. Baste with the lemon mixture. Grill for 25 to 30 minutes or until the chicken is cooked through, basting every 5 minutes. Discard any leftover basting mixture.

Yield: 8 servings

Runnin' Rebel Chicken

This recipe was provided by Coach Bill Bayno.

1 (10-ounce) can cream of mushroom soup
1/8 teaspoon cayenne pepper, or to taste
1 (3-ounce) can French-fried onions
4 chicken breasts

Combine the soup, cayenne pepper and about 1 cup of the French-fried onions in a bowl and mix well. Coat a 9×12-inch baking dish with nonstick cooking spray.

Arrange the chicken in the baking dish. Spread the soup mixture over the chicken. Cover the dish with foil.

Bake at 350 degrees for 45 minutes or until the chicken is cooked through, basting the chicken frequently while baking. Remove the foil and sprinkle with the remaining onions. Bake, uncovered, at 400 degrees for 15 minutes or until golden brown.

Yield: 4 servings

Bill Bayno

Bill Bayno is the tenth basketball coach of the UNLV Runnin' Rebels in the 41-year history of the program and has guided the Rebels to postseason play the last three seasons. He came to UNLV from UMass, where he served seven years as an assistant coach under John Calipari. Bayno played a major role in UMass's rise in national prominence, as the Minutemen made five consecutive trips to the NCAA Tournament. Bayno started his collegiate coaching career as P. J. Carlesimo's first graduate assistant at Seton Hall. Bayno joined Larry Brown's staff at Kansas as a graduate assistant and helped take the Jayhawks to the NCAA Sweet Sixteen. Bayno left Kansas to become the top assistant under Gary Edwards at Baptist College in Charleston, South Carolina, where he remained for a year before going to UMass.

Chicken Madeira

4 boneless skinless chicken breasts
3/4 cup flour
1 teaspoon salt
3/4 teaspoon pepper
8 tablespoons (1 stick) butter
1/2 cup madeira
1/4 cup water
1 tablespoon fresh lemon juice
1/2 teaspoon minced garlic
3 tablespoons butter
1 pound fresh mushrooms, sliced

Cut each piece of chicken into halves and pound to a thickness of 1/8 inch. Mix the flour, salt and pepper in a shallow dish. Coat the chicken in the flour mixture. Melt 4 tablespoons of the butter in a skillet over medium heat. Add half the chicken and cook for 2 to 3 minutes per side or until lightly browned. Remove the chicken to a 9×13-inch baking dish.

Melt 4 tablespoons butter in the skillet and brown the remaining chicken. Remove to the baking dish. Add the wine and water to the skillet. Cook over medium heat, scraping up browned bits. Add the lemon juice and garlic. Cook for 2 minutes or until the liquid is syrupy. Pour over the chicken in the baking dish. Add 3 tablespoons butter to the skillet. Add the mushrooms and sauté until tender. Spoon over the chicken. Cover the baking dish with foil. Bake at 350 degrees for 40 minutes. Serve the chicken garnished with chopped parsley and cherry tomatoes.

NOTE: This dish can be made up to 24 hours ahead. Cover and chill. Bake just before serving.

Yield: 8 servings

Spicy Garlic Chicken Pizza

1/4 cup sliced green onions
2 garlic cloves, minced
2 tablespoons rice vinegar or white vinegar
2 tablespoons soy sauce
1 tablespoon olive oil
1/2 teaspoon crushed red pepper, or
    1/4 teaspoon cayenne pepper
1/4 teaspoon black pepper
12 ounces boneless skinless chicken breasts,
    cut into 1/2-inch pieces
1 tablespoon cornstarch
1 tablespoon olive oil
1 (16-ounce) Boboli Italian bread shell
1/2 cup shredded Monterey Jack cheese
1/2 cup shredded mozzarella cheese
1/4 cup sliced green onions
2 tablespoons pine nuts or sliced almonds

Combine 1/4 cup green onions, garlic, vinegar, soy sauce,
1 tablespoon olive oil, red pepper and black pepper in a bowl
and mix well. Add the chicken and stir to coat. Let stand for
30 minutes at room temperature. Drain and reserve the marinade.
Stir the cornstarch into the marinade.

Heat 1 tablespoon olive oil in a large skillet and add the chicken.
Sauté for 3 minutes or until cooked through. Add the reserved
marinade to the skillet. Cook until thick and bubbly, stirring
constantly. Spoon the chicken mixture evenly onto the bread
shell. Sprinkle with the Monterey Jack cheese and mozzarella
cheese. Bake at 400 degrees for 12 minutes. Top with 1/4 cup
green onions and pine nuts. Bake for 2 minutes longer.
Serve hot.

Yield: 6 servings

Silver and Gold

*Nevada is an important
mineral-producing state,
leading the nation in
production of gold, barite,
silver, and mercury.
Natural resources and
minerals in the state
include gold, silver, copper,
lead, zinc, tungsten,
uranium, manganese,
titanium, iron, mercury,
opal, molybdenum, barite,
diatomite, magnetite, talc,
gypsum, dolomite, lime,
turquoise, brucite, fluorspar,
antimony, perlite, pumice,
salt, and sulfur oilshale.
Sixty-one percent of the
United States' gold and
10 percent of the world's
total output has been mined
from Nevada. More than
6,000,000 ounces mined each
year makes Nevada the largest
gold-producing state in the
nation. The largest-ever gold
nugget found in Nevada
weighs 25 pounds and is
displayed in the Golden Nugget
Hotel. Gypsum is mined
extensively in the Las Vegas
area and is later manufactured
into wallboard or plasterboard.*

Chutney Peanut Chicken

1/2 cup peach or mango chutney
1 cup cocktail peanuts, crushed or finely chopped
4 boneless skinless chicken breasts

Finely chop any large pieces of fruit in the chutney. Place the chutney in a shallow dish. Place the peanuts in a separate shallow dish. Dip the chicken in the chutney and then in the peanuts to coat. Arrange the coated chicken in a lightly oiled baking dish. Bake at 400 degrees for 25 to 35 minutes or until the chicken is cooked through. Turn the chicken once during baking. Serve with white rice.

NOTE: Crush the peanuts by placing in a plastic bag and hammering with a kitchen mallet or finely chop them in a food processor.

Yield: 4 servings

Spicy Barbecued Chicken

1 cup each vegetable oil and vinegar
1/4 cup salt
2 tablespoons ground black pepper
1 tablespoon each crushed red pepper, prepared mustard and
    Worcestershire sauce
1 teaspoon hot pepper sauce
1 teaspoon paprika
3 to 4 pounds chicken pieces

Combine the vegetable oil, vinegar, salt, black pepper, red pepper, mustard, Worcestershire sauce, hot pepper sauce and paprika in a large bowl and mix well. Add the chicken and stir to coat. Cover and marinate in the refrigerator for 8 to 24 hours. Turn the chicken once or twice during marinating. Remove the chicken and discard the marinade. Grill or broil until cooked through.

NOTE: Skinless chicken will absorb more of the marinade flavor.

Yield: 6 to 8 servings

Chicken Cheese Puffs

3 ounces cream cheese, softened
2 tablespoons butter, softened
2 tablespoons milk
2 cups chopped cooked chicken
$1/4$ teaspoon salt
$1/8$ teaspoon pepper
1 (8-count) can refrigerated crescent rolls

Combine the cream cheese, butter and milk in a bowl. Beat with an electric mixer at medium speed until smooth. Stir in the chicken, salt and pepper. Unroll the dough and separate into 4 rectangles. Press the perforations to seal.

Spoon $1/2$ cup of the chicken mixture onto the center of each rectangle. Bring the 4 corners of the dough over the filling and twist. Pinch the edges to seal. Place on an ungreased baking sheet. Bake at 350 degrees for 20 to 25 minutes or until golden brown.

NOTE: You may substitute puff pastry for the crescent roll dough and add chopped vegetables and $1/2$ cup shredded sharp Cheddar cheese. Baking time and/or temperature may need to be adjusted.

Yield: 4 servings

Red Pepper Sauce

1 large red bell pepper, seeded, chopped
1/2 yellow onion, chopped
1/2 jalapeño chile, seeded, finely chopped
Juice of 1 lemon
1 tablespoon olive oil
Salt and pepper to taste

Combine the bell pepper, onion, jalapeño, lemon juice and olive oil in a saucepan and mix well. Cover and cook over low heat until the bell pepper and onion are tender. Purée in a blender or food processor until smooth. Season with salt and pepper. Pour into a bowl and serve as a condiment for barbecued meats, chicken and fish.

Yield: about 1 cup

Grilled Mojave Quail

8 quail
1/3 cup butter, melted
1/3 cup soy sauce
1/8 teaspoon Worcestershire sauce, or to taste
1/2 teaspoon dried sage

Rinse the quail and pat dry with a paper towel. Whisk the butter, soy sauce, Worcestershire sauce and sage in a small bowl. Grill the quail over a low to medium flame. Turn several times and baste with the sauce during grilling. Grill for 8 minutes or just until cooked through. Do not overcook.

Yield: 4 servings

Cornish Game Hens with Amaretto Stuffing

This dish is pictured on page 96.

1/2 cup amaretto
1 cup dried cherries or cranberries
1/4 cup (1/2 stick) butter or margarine
1/2 cup chopped onion
1/3 cup chopped celery
4 cups bread cubes or stuffing mix
1 egg, lightly beaten
1 cup chicken broth
Salt and pepper to taste
4 Cornish game hens, or 1 (2- to 3-pound) chicken
Honey Glaze (at right)

Mix the liqueur and dried cherries in a small bowl. Let stand for 15 minutes or longer. Melt the butter in a skillet. Add the onion and celery and sauté until tender. Place the onion mixture in a bowl. Add the bread cubes, egg, chicken broth and undrained cherries. Season with salt and pepper. Toss until well mixed. Spoon the stuffing into the cavities of the hens.

Place the hens in a 9×13-inch baking pan. Bake at 350 degrees for 20 minutes. Baste with some of the Honey Glaze. Bake for 55 to 65 minutes or until cooked through, basting with Honey Glaze every 10 to 15 minutes.

Yield: 4 servings

Honey Glaze

1/4 cup honey
1/4 cup cherry juice or cranberry juice
1/4 cup amaretto
1/4 cup packed light brown sugar
2 tablespoons butter or margarine
1/4 cup Chinese five-spice powder

Combine the honey, cherry juice, amaretto, brown sugar, butter and five-spice powder in a saucepan. Heat until the butter is melted, stirring occasionally.

Yield: about 1 cup

Oyster Stew

36 shucked oysters, with their liquor
6 cups heavy cream
8 ounces sharp Cheddar or Monterey Jack cheese, shredded
Green parts only of 1 bunch green onions, chopped
1 (2-ounce) jar pimentos, chopped
Salt and white pepper to taste
1 pound fresh spinach, chopped
2 tablespoons grated Parmesan cheese

Drain the oysters in a sieve and reserve the liquor. Add enough water to the reserved liquor to measure 1 cup. Rinse the oysters; drain and set aside.

Combine the oyster liquor mixture and the cream in a large saucepan. Bring to a boil and reduce the heat. Simmer for 10 minutes. Add the Cheddar cheese, green onions and pimentos and cook until the cheese melts, stirring occasionally. Season with salt and pepper.

Stir the spinach, Parmesan cheese and oysters into the pimento mixture in the saucepan. Simmer for 2 minutes or until the edges of the oysters start to curl. Spoon into bowls and garnish with caviar.

Yield: 4 to 6 servings

Macadamia-Encrusted Escolar

This recipe was provided by chef Terrence Fong.

1 cup panko flakes (see Note)
1/4 cup finely chopped unsalted macadamia nuts
8 (4-ounce) escolar fillets (see Note)
Salt and pepper to taste
2 tablespoons grapeseed oil
White Corn Cakes (below)
Peanut sauce

Mix the panko flakes and macadamia nuts in a shallow bowl. Season the fish fillets with salt and pepper and coat with the nut mixture. Heat the grapeseed oil in a skillet and add the fillets. Brown the fish on 1 side. Place browned side up in a baking dish. Bake at 350 degrees for 7 minutes. Serve with White Corn Cakes and peanut sauce.

NOTE: Panko is Japanese bread crumbs. Escolar is a type of mackerel.

Yield: 8 servings

White Corn Cakes

Kernels of 6 ears roasted white corn
1 roasted red bell pepper, peeled, seeded, chopped
1/4 bunch cilantro, chopped
3 tablespoons sugar
3/4 cup flour
2 egg yolks
Salt and pepper to taste
1/2 cup grapeseed oil

Mix the corn, bell pepper, cilantro, sugar, flour, egg yolks, salt and pepper in a bowl. Fold in the grapeseed oil. Chill for 15 minutes. Shape into cakes and place on a greased baking sheet. Bake at 450 degrees for 20 minutes or until golden brown. Serve hot.

Yield: 8 servings

Terrence Fong

Terrence Fong is the chef de cuisine at Gatsby's in the MGM Grand. Gatsby's is known for quality, from the moment you sit down in the plush leather armchairs at tables shining with Riedel Crystal wine glasses, Christofle silver, and china from Boch and Limoges. Fong uses nothing but the best: farm-raised salmon, ostrich, and extravagant Japanese Kobe beef. Sample Chef Fong's Kobe steak and you will be an addict for life.

Smoked Salmon Pizza

The recipes on these two pages were provided by chef Wolfgang Puck.

Pizza Dough (page 141)
Olive oil
Thinly sliced red onion
1/4 cup (or more) Dill Cream (below)
Thinly sliced cold smoked salmon

Place the Pizza Dough on a floured surface. Flatten the dough with your
fingers to make a circle. Lift the dough and gently stretch until the circle is
8 inches in diameter and thicker around the rim. Place the crust on a baking
sheet or hot pizza stone. Brush with olive oil. Top generously with red onion.
Bake at 450 degrees for 5 to 6 minutes or until golden brown. Spread the Dill
Cream over the onions. Top with a layer of smoked salmon. Cut with a large
knife. Garnish with chopped chives and caviar. Serve immediately.

Yield: 2 servings

Dill Cream

2 cups sour cream
3 tablespoons chopped fresh dill
2 tablespoons finely chopped shallots
3 tablespoons (or more) lemon juice
Salt and pepper to taste

Combine the sour cream, dill, shallots and lemon juice in a bowl and
mix well. Season with salt and pepper. Cover and chill.

Yield: about 2 cups

Pizza Dough

1 envelope dry yeast
1/4 cup warm (110-degree) water
1 teaspoon salt
1 tablespoon honey
2 tablespoons olive oil
3/4 cup cool water
3 cups flour

Dissolve the yeast in the warm water in a small bowl. Let stand for 10 minutes. Combine the salt, honey, olive oil and cool water in a measuring cup or small bowl and mix well. Place the flour in a food processor container. Add the cool water mixture in a stream with the motor running. Add the dissolved yeast with the motor running. Process until the dough forms a ball. Add additional flour if the dough is sticky.

Place the dough on a lightly floured surface and knead until smooth. Place in a greased bowl and turn to coat the surface. Cover and let stand for 30 minutes. Divide the dough into 4 balls. Place the balls on a large plate and cover with a damp towel. Store in the refrigerator until ready to use. Remove from the refrigerator 1 hour before baking to allow the dough to come to room temperature.

Yield: 4 (7- to 8-inch) pizza crusts

Wolfgang Puck

Wolfgang Puck first made his mark as one of an influential breed of young chef-restaurateurs who launched new trends in California cuisine by expertly blending fresh local ingredients with classical French technique. Puck has opened several restaurants in Las Vegas resorts. His restaurant, Spago, known for its high-energy atmosphere and his trademark gourmet pizzas, attracts a "glitter to gourmet" Las Vegas crowd.

Mustard-Glazed Salmon

2 tablespoons butter
2 tablespoons light brown sugar
3 tablespoons Creole mustard
2 tablespoons Dijon mustard
1 garlic clove, minced
8 (5- to 8-ounce) salmon fillets

Melt the butter in a saucepan. Stir in the brown sugar, Creole mustard, Dijon mustard and garlic. Remove from the heat. Pat the salmon dry with paper towels. Dip the salmon in the mustard mixture to coat both sides. Grill 4 to 6 inches from the coals or broil 6 inches from the heat source. Cook until the salmon is browned and becoming opaque at the thickest part. Baste frequently with the mustard mixture while cooking.

Yield: 8 servings

Salted Black Bean Jus

1 tablespoon vegetable oil
1 tablespoon minced garlic
1 cup sherry
2 tablespoons finely chopped salted black beans
   (see Note, page 143)
4 cups vegetable stock
1 1/2 tablespoons cornstarch
1/4 cup cold water

Heat the vegetable oil in a 2-quart saucepan. Add the garlic and sauté until tender. Stir in the sherry and cook until the liquid is reduced by 1/2. Stir in the salted black beans and simmer for 2 minutes. Add the vegetable stock and bring to a boil. Dissolve the cornstarch in the cold water in a small cup. Add to the saucepan. Simmer over low heat for 10 minutes, stirring occasionally. Keep warm.

Yield: 4 1/2 cups

Steamed Sea Bass

This recipe and the recipe for Salted Black Bean Jus were provided by chef Michael Ty.

6 (7- to 8-ounce) sea bass fillets
6 slices gingerroot
1 tablespoon salted black bean paste (see Note)
1 tablespoon vegetable oil
1½ teaspoons minced shallots
12 shiitake mushrooms, stems removed
Salt and white pepper to taste
1 bunch green onions
18 baby carrots
9 baby bok choy, blanched, cooled, quartered
Salted Black Bean Jus (page 142)

Place the sea bass fillets in a baking dish. Top each with a slice of gingerroot and a small amount of black bean paste. Cover and chill. Heat the vegetable oil in a skillet. Add the shallots and mushrooms and sauté until tender. Season with salt and white pepper. Set aside and keep warm. Julienne 2 green onions and place in ice water in a bowl. Line a steamer basket with the remaining green onions. Place the sea bass fillets on top of the green onions and add the carrots.

Steam for 4 minutes. Add the blanched bok choy to the steamer. Steam for 4 to 6 minutes or until the fish is cooked through. Arrange the sea bass, carrots and bok choy on 6 soup plates. Top with the mushroom mixture. Ladle Salted Black Bean Jus onto each plate and garnish with the julienned green onions.

NOTE: Salted black beans are fermented black soybeans. They can be found at Asian markets.

Yield: 6 servings

Michael Ty

Chef Michael Ty's gourmet fare can be sampled at Lawry's The Prime Rib.

Festive Shrimp

1/3 cup butter
2 tablespoons olive oil
2 shallots, minced
2 garlic cloves, minced
1 pound uncooked medium shrimp, peeled, deveined
3 small plum tomatoes, seeded, chopped
1/2 teaspoon dried basil
1/2 teaspoon dried oregano
1/2 teaspoon salt
1/2 teaspoon pepper
1/2 cup dry sherry
3 bunches fresh spinach, rinsed, drained, stems removed
1/2 cup heavy cream
Hot cooked rice or pasta

Melt the butter with the olive oil in a large skillet over medium-low heat. Add the shallots and garlic. Sauté for 5 minutes. Add the shrimp, tomatoes, basil, oregano, salt and pepper. Sauté until the shrimp begin to turn pink.

Add the sherry and spinach to the shrimp mixture. Cook, covered, for 5 minutes or until the spinach wilts, stirring occasionally. Stir in the cream. Cook until heated through, stirring frequently. Serve over hot cooked rice or pasta.

Yield: 4 servings

"Sincerely" Swordfish

This recipe was provided by Phyllis McGuire.

Juice of 3 limes
1/2 cup white wine
1/2 cup heavy cream
Salt and pepper to taste
1/2 cup (1 stick) butter, cut into pieces
6 (1-inch-thick) swordfish steaks
1/4 cup virgin olive oil
1/3 cup chopped green onions
1/3 cup chopped cilantro

Combine the lime juice and wine in a saucepan. Cook over medium heat until reduced by 2/3. Stir in the cream. Cook until reduced again by 2/3. Season with salt and pepper. Whisk in the butter. Cook until the butter is melted, whisking constantly. Set aside and keep warm.

Season the swordfish with salt. Heat the olive oil in a skillet until very hot. Add the swordfish. Cook over high heat for 3 minutes per side or until the outside is very browned and the inside is slightly pink. Stir the green onions and 1/3 cup cilantro into the lime sauce. Spoon the sauce onto serving plates. Top with the cooked swordfish steak and garnish with chopped cilantro.

Yield: 6 servings

Phyllis McGuire

Known as "the one in the middle" of the famed McGuire sisters, Phyllis burst onto the music scene in 1952 when the group won a spot on the Arthur Godfrey Talent Scouts show. The rest is music history. Just as she became a fixture on the Las Vegas stage, Phyllis has also become an icon on the city's social scene with her appearances and contributions.

Spicy Grilled Shrimp

1/4 cup vegetable oil
1 teaspoon salt
1/2 teaspoon pepper
1 garlic clove, minced
1/3 cup vinegar
1/3 cup chili sauce
2 tablespoons Worcestershire sauce
1/8 teaspoon hot pepper sauce
1/2 cup finely chopped fresh parsley
2 pounds uncooked medium shrimp, peeled, deveined

Mix the vegetable oil, salt, pepper, garlic, vinegar, chili sauce, Worcestershire sauce, hot pepper sauce and parsley in a bowl. Add the shrimp and stir to coat. Cover and chill for 1 to 2 hours. Remove the shrimp from the marinade, reserving the marinade. Thread the shrimp onto skewers. Place on an oiled grill rack 4 to 6 inches above the coals. Grill for 4 minutes. Baste with the reserved marinade and turn the skewers over. Grill for 4 minutes or until cooked through.

Yield: 6 servings

Vegetable Shrimp Stir-Fry

6 ounces snow peas, trimmed
6 green onions, sliced
2 red bell peppers, seeded, sliced
1 tablespoon virgin olive oil
1 pound uncooked medium shrimp, peeled, deveined
4 ounces mushrooms, quartered
2 tablespoons soy sauce
1 tablespoon seasoned rice vinegar
1 teaspoon sesame oil

Stir-fry the peas, green onions and bell peppers in the heated olive oil in a large skillet or wok over medium-high heat for 2 minutes. Add the shrimp. Stir-fry for 2 minutes or until the shrimp turn pink. Add the mushrooms. Stir-fry until the mushrooms are tender and most of the liquid evaporates. Add the remaining ingredients. Cook until heated through, stirring constantly.

Yield: 4 servings

Shrimp Scampi

3 tablespoons butter
2 tablespoons minced garlic
1^1/2 pounds uncooked shrimp, peeled, deveined
^{1}/4 cup dry white wine
^{1}/2 cup tomato sauce
1 cup heavy cream
^{1}/2 teaspoon dried basil
1 teaspoon dried oregano
2 egg yolks
^{1}/4 cup heavy cream
Salt and pepper to taste
Hot cooked pasta
2 tablespoons chopped fresh parsley

Melt the butter in a skillet. Add the garlic and sauté for 1 minute. Add the shrimp. Sauté until the shrimp turn pink. Add the wine and tomato sauce. Cook for 1 minute, stirring constantly. Stir in 1 cup cream, basil and oregano.

Beat the egg yolks with ^{1}/4 cup cream in a small bowl. Add to the skillet. Cook until heated through, stirring constantly. Do not boil. Season with salt and pepper. Serve over hot cooked pasta. Sprinkle with the parsley. Serve with Corona Pinot Grigio.

NOTE: If fresh parsley is not available and dried parsley is used, add and cook with the basil and oregano.

Yield: 6 servings

Grand Canyon

The Grand Canyon is a frequent destination for Las Vegas visitors, by both car and plane. It is about 300 miles and 1^1/2 hours by plane from Las Vegas. The park encompasses 277 miles of the Colorado River and adjacent lands. It is one of the most magnificent examples of erosion anywhere. The views from both the north and south rim are incomparable.

Grand Finales

Desserts

pictured at left: Neon Lights Delight
(recipe on page 185)

Lazy Daisy Cake

2 eggs
1 cup sugar
1 teaspoon vanilla extract
1 cup flour
1 teaspoon baking powder
1/4 teaspoon salt
1/2 cup hot milk
2 tablespoons butter, melted
1/4 cup packed brown sugar
3 tablespoons butter, melted
1/4 cup heavy cream
1/2 cup flaked coconut

Beat the eggs in a mixing bowl. Add the sugar and vanilla and beat well. Beat in the flour, baking powder and salt. Add the milk and 2 tablespoons melted butter and beat well.

Pour the batter into a greased and floured 8×9-inch cake pan. Bake at 300 degrees for 45 minutes or until a wooden pick inserted near the center comes out clean. Cool slightly on a wire rack.

Mix the brown sugar, 3 tablespoons melted butter, cream and coconut in a bowl. Spread on top of the baked cake. Broil 4 inches from the heat source for 1 minute or until bubbly. Let cool before cutting.

Yield: 6 to 8 servings

"Let Them Eat Cake"

This recipe was provided by Senator Harry Reid.

2 cups flour
2 cups sugar
1 cup (2 sticks) butter
1/4 cup (or more) baking cocoa
1 cup water
1 teaspoon baking soda
1/2 cup buttermilk
2 eggs, beaten
1 teaspoon vanilla extract
Creamy Chocolate Frosting (below)

Mix the flour and sugar in a large bowl. Combine the butter, baking cocoa and water in a saucepan. Bring to a boil. Pour over the flour mixture and stir to mix well. Mix the baking soda with the buttermilk in a small bowl. Stir into the cake batter. Stir in the eggs and vanilla. Pour the batter into a greased 10×15-inch cake pan. Bake at 350 degrees for 30 minutes or until a wooden pick inserted near the center comes out clean. Cool slightly on a wire rack. Pour warm Creamy Chocolate Frosting over the warm cake. Let cool before cutting.

Yield: 16 servings

Creamy Chocolate Frosting

1/2 cup (1 stick) butter
3 tablespoons (or more) baking cocoa
5 tablespoons milk
1 (1-pound) package confectioners' sugar
1 teaspoon vanilla extract
1/2 cup chopped pecans

Heat the butter, baking cocoa and milk in a saucepan until the butter melts. Remove from the heat. Beat in the confectioners' sugar, vanilla and pecans. Let cool slightly.

Yield: about 3 cups

Harry Reid

Senator Harry Reid comes from the rural mining town of Searchlight, Nevada, where he learned the fundamental values of hard work and honesty that remain his guiding principles. Reid is currently serving his third term in the U.S. Senate, and in 1998 he was elected Minority Whip. In addition to his leadership duties, Senator Reid also sits on the Appropriations Committee, Environment and Public Works Committee, Ethics Committee, Indian Affairs Committee, and Special Committee on Aging. He and his wife, Landra, are dedicated to serving Nevada.

151

Oatmeal Chocolate Chip Cake

1³/4 cups boiling water
1 cup rolled oats
1 cup packed brown sugar
1 cup sugar
¹/2 cup (1 stick) margarine
2 eggs
1³/4 cups flour
1 teaspoon baking soda
¹/2 teaspoon salt
1 tablespoon baking cocoa
1 cup chocolate chips
³/4 cup chopped pecans or walnuts
1 cup chocolate chips

Pour the boiling water over the oats in a bowl and let stand for 10 minutes. Combine the brown sugar, sugar and margarine in a large bowl. Add the oatmeal mixture, stirring until the margarine is melted. Beat in the eggs. Sift the flour, baking soda, salt and baking cocoa into a bowl. Add the dry ingredients to the oatmeal mixture and mix well. Stir in 1 cup chocolate chips and the pecans. Pour the batter into a greased and floured 9×13-inch cake pan.

Bake at 350 degrees for 35 to 40 minutes or until a wooden pick inserted near the center comes out clean. Remove to a wire rack. Sprinkle with 1 cup chocolate chips. Let stand for a few minutes to allow the chocolate chips to melt. Spread the melted chips on the cake. Serve warm.

Yield: 12 servings

Italian Coconut Cream Cake

1/2 cup (1 stick) butter, softened
1/2 cup vegetable shortening
2 cups sugar
5 egg yolks
2 cups flour
1 teaspoon baking powder
1 cup buttermilk
2 cups flaked coconut
1/2 cup chopped pecans or walnuts
1 teaspoon vanilla extract
5 egg whites, stiffly beaten
Cream Cheese Frosting (at right)
Flaked coconut

Beat the butter, shortening and sugar in a bowl until light and fluffy. Beat in the egg yolks. Mix the flour and baking powder in a small bowl. Add to the butter mixture and mix well. Beat in the buttermilk, 2 cups coconut, pecans and vanilla. Fold in the egg whites. Pour the batter into 3 greased and floured 9-inch round cake pans.

Bake at 350 degrees for 30 to 35 minutes or until a wooden pick inserted near the center comes out clean. Cool in the pans for 10 minutes. Invert the layers onto wire racks. Let cool completely. Spread Cream Cheese Frosting between the layers and over the side and top. Sprinkle with additional coconut.

Yield: 8 to 10 servings

Cream Cheese Frosting

3 ounces cream cheese, softened
1/2 cup (1 stick) butter, softened
1 (1-pound) package confectioners' sugar
1 teaspoon vanilla extract

Beat the cream cheese and butter in a mixing bowl with an electric mixer until light and fluffy. Beat in the confectioners' sugar gradually. Add the vanilla and beat until smooth.

Yield: about 2 1/2 cups

Rum Cake

1 (2-layer) package pudding-recipe yellow cake mix
4 eggs
1/2 cup water
1/2 cup rum
1/2 cup maraschino cherries
1/2 cup chopped pecans
1 cup sugar
1/2 cup (1 stick) butter
1/4 cup water
1/4 to 1/2 cup rum

Combine the cake mix, eggs, 1/2 cup water and 1/2 cup rum in a mixing bowl. Beat with an electric mixer until light and fluffy. Arrange the maraschino cherries and pecans in the bottom of a greased and floured 10-cup bundt pan. Pour the cake batter over the cherries and pecans. Bake at 350 degrees for 50 to 60 minutes or until a wooden pick inserted near the center comes out clean. Let cool on a wire rack for 10 minutes.

Combine the sugar, butter and 1/4 cup water in a saucepan. Bring to a boil and boil for 4 minutes, stirring constantly. Remove from the heat and stir in 1/4 to 1/2 cup rum. Pour the rum syrup over the cake. Loosen the side and center of the cake from the pan to allow the syrup to seep down the side and under the cake. Let cool completely. Invert onto a serving plate.

Yield: 8 servings

Greek Walnut Cake

1 cup flour
1¹/₂ teaspoons baking powder
¹/₂ teaspoon cinnamon
¹/₄ teaspoon salt
¹/₈ teaspoon ground nutmeg
³/₄ cup (1¹/₂ sticks) butter, softened
³/₄ cup sugar
3 eggs
2 tablespoons grated lemon peel
¹/₄ cup milk
1¹/₂ cups finely chopped walnuts
1 cup Honey Syrup (at right)

Sift the flour, baking powder, cinnamon, salt and nutmeg into a bowl. Beat the butter and sugar in a mixing bowl with an electric mixer until light and fluffy. Add the eggs 1 at a time, beating well after each addition. Stir in the lemon peel. Add the milk alternately with the dry ingredients, mixing well after each addition. Stir in the walnuts.

Pour the batter into a greased and floured 8×8-inch cake pan. Bake at 350 degrees for 35 minutes or until the top springs back when lightly pressed. Let cool on a wire rack for 10 minutes. Pour cooled Honey Syrup over the cake, letting the syrup soak in before adding more. Cut the cake when cool.

NOTE: You can pour hot syrup over the cooled cake if preferred.

Yield: 6 servings

Honey Syrup

1 small lemon
1 cup sugar
1 cup water
1 (2-inch) stick of
  cinnamon
2 whole cloves
1 cup honey
1¹/₂ tablespoons freshly
  squeezed lemon juice
1 tablespoon brandy
  (optional)

Remove the peel from the lemon, being careful to remove only the thin yellow part. Combine the lemon peel, sugar, water, cinnamon and cloves in a heavy saucepan. Bring to a boil and reduce the heat. Cook without stirring for 25 minutes or until the mixture is syrupy and registers 230 degrees on a candy thermometer. Remove from the heat and stir in the honey. Strain into a 2-cup measuring cup. Stir in the lemon juice and brandy.

Yield: about 2 cups

Five-Flavor Pound Cake

1 cup (2 sticks) butter, softened
1/2 cup vegetable shortening
3 cups sugar
5 eggs, beaten
3 cups cake flour, sifted
1/2 teaspoon baking powder
1 cup milk
1 teaspoon rum extract
1 teaspoon butter extract
1 teaspoon lemon extract
1 teaspoon vanilla extract
1 teaspoon coconut extract
1 cup sugar
1/2 cup water
1 teaspoon rum extract
1 teaspoon butter extract
1 teaspoon lemon extract
1 teaspoon vanilla extract
1 teaspoon coconut extract

For the cake, beat the butter, shortening and 3 cups sugar in a mixing bowl with an electric mixer until light and fluffy. Beat in the eggs. Sift the flour and baking powder into a bowl. Add to the butter mixture alternately with the milk, beating well after each addition. Beat in 1 teaspoon each rum, butter, lemon, vanilla and coconut extract.

Pour the batter into a greased and floured 10-inch tube pan. Bake at 350 degrees for 1 1/2 hours or until a wooden pick inserted near the center comes out clean. Cool in the pan for 10 minutes. Invert onto a wire rack. Let cool completely.

For the frosting, combine 1 cup sugar, water and 1 teaspoon each rum, butter, lemon, vanilla and coconut extract in a saucepan. Bring to a boil and cook until the sugar dissolves, stirring constantly. Remove from the heat and let cool slightly. Pour on the cake and let run down the sides.

Yield: 12 servings

Pineapple Upside-Down Cake

This recipe was provided by chef Stanton Ho.

1 fresh medium pineapple, peeled, cored, finely chopped
6 tablespoons unsalted butter
1 cup packed brown sugar
6 tablespoons unsalted butter
3 tablespoons dark rum
1 2/3 cups flour
2 teaspoons baking powder
1 teaspoon salt
1/2 cup (1 stick) butter, softened
1 cup sugar
2 eggs
1 cup sour cream
1 tablespoon dark rum

Spread the pineapple in twelve 4-ounce buttered muffin cups. Combine 6 tablespoons butter and the brown sugar in a saucepan. Bring to a boil, stirring constantly. Stir in 6 tablespoons butter gradually. Cook until thick and creamy, stirring constantly. Stir in 3 tablespoons dark rum and continue cooking for a few minutes. Remove from the heat and spoon about 2 tablespoons over the pineapple in each muffin cup.

Sift the flour, baking powder and salt into a bowl. Beat 1/2 cup butter and the sugar in a mixing bowl until light and fluffy. Add the eggs 1 at a time, beating well after each addition. Beat in the sour cream. Beat in 1 tablespoon dark rum. Add the dry ingredients gradually, beating well after each addition. Fill the muffin cups 1/2 full with batter.

Bake at 375 degrees for 15 to 20 minutes or until a wooden pick inserted near the center of the cakes comes out clean. Cool on a wire rack. Invert onto a serving plate when completely cooled.

Yield: 12 servings

Stanton Ho

Stanton Ho is the Executive Pastry Chef at the Las Vegas Hilton.

Tropical Fruitcake

3 cups flour
2 cups sugar
1 tablespoon baking powder
1¹/₂ teaspoons salt
1¹/₄ cups vegetable oil
1 cup crushed pineapple
1 teaspoon vanilla extract
1 teaspoon pineapple extract (optional)
3 eggs
2 cups finely chopped apples
1 (8-ounce) package finely chopped dates
1¹/₃ cups flaked coconut
1 cup chopped walnuts
1 cup miniature marshmallows
1 cup confectioners' sugar (optional)
3 to 4 tablespoons fruit juice or milk (optional)

Combine the flour, sugar, baking powder, salt, vegetable oil, pineapple, vanilla, pineapple extract and eggs in a large bowl. Beat with an electric mixer at medium speed for 3 minutes. Stir in the apples, dates, coconut, walnuts and marshmallows. Pour the batter into a greased and floured 10-inch bundt pan or tube pan.

Bake at 325 degrees for 1 hour and 20 minutes to 1 hour and 30 minutes or until a wooden pick inserted near the center comes out clean. Let cool in the pan for 15 minutes. Invert onto a wire rack and let cool completely. Beat the confectioners' sugar and fruit juice in a bowl until smooth. Drizzle over the cooled cake.

Yield: 12 servings

Crème de Menthe Torte

1 cup fine chocolate wafer cookie crumbs
2 tablespoons butter, melted
1 1/4 cups half-and-half
2 1/2 cups packed miniature marshmallows
1/2 cup green crème de menthe
1/3 cup white crème de cacao
6 drops (about) green food coloring
2 egg whites
3 tablespoons sugar
1 1/2 cups whipping cream

Combine the chocolate cookie crumbs and melted butter in a bowl. Mix well. Press into the bottom and 2 inches up the side of an 8- or 9-inch springform pan. Set aside.

Combine the half-and-half and marshmallows in a 3-quart saucepan. Cook until the marshmallows are melted, stirring constantly. Set the pan in cold water and stir until the mixture is cool. Remove the pan from the water. Stir in the crème de menthe, crème de cacao and food coloring. Chill until the mixture begins to thicken.

Beat the egg whites in a bowl until soft peaks form. Add the sugar to the egg whites gradually, beating constantly until stiff peaks form. Whip the cream in a large bowl until stiff peaks form. Fold the cooled marshmallow mixture and beaten egg whites into the whipped cream. Pour into the prepared crust. Cover and freeze for 8 hours or up to 5 days.

Place the torte on a serving plate. Loosen from the side of the pan with a sharp knife and remove the side of the pan. Garnish with chocolate curls.

Yield: 6 to 8 servings

Four-of-a-Kind Cocktail

1/4 cup vodka
2 tablespoons Irish cream liqueur
2 tablespoons chocolate liqueur
2 tablespoons sweetened condensed milk
1 tablespoon amaretto
1/2 cup crushed ice

Combine the vodka, Irish cream, chocolate liqueur, condensed milk, amaretto and ice in a blender container. Blend at low speed until creamy. Pour into a glass.

Yield: 1 serving

Swiss Almond Tea Wafers

1 1/2 cups sliced almonds, lightly toasted
1/2 cup sugar
2 teaspoons grated orange peel
1/2 cup (1 stick) butter, softened
1 egg
2 egg yolks
2 tablespoons amaretto
2 1/4 cups flour
1/4 teaspoon salt
1 egg yolk
1 tablespoon water
2 tablespoons sugar
Silver candy balls (dragées)

Process the almonds, 1/2 cup sugar and orange peel in a food processor until finely ground. Cream the butter in a mixing bowl until light and fluffy. Beat in the almond mixture. Add the egg, 2 egg yolks and amaretto and beat well. Combine the flour and salt in a bowl. Add to the creamed mixture and beat until mixed.

Shape the dough into a ball. Cover with plastic wrap and chill until firm. Place the dough between 2 sheets of waxed paper. Roll the dough to a thickness of 1/4 inch. Turn the dough over and loosen the paper occasionally while rolling. Cut the dough with a 2-inch cookie cutter. Re-roll and cut the dough scraps. Place the cookies 1/2 inch apart on greased and floured cookie sheets. Mix 1 egg yolk with the water. Brush on the cookies. Sprinkle lightly with 2 tablespoons sugar and decorate with the silver candy balls.

Bake at 350 degrees for 15 to 18 minutes or until the cookies are browned around the edges and golden brown in the center. Remove to wire racks to cool. Store in an airtight container for up to 1 week.

Yield: 5 1/2 dozen

Superlative Chocolate Chip Cookies

1 cup (2 sticks) butter, softened
1/2 cup vegetable shortening
1 1/3 cups sugar
1 cup packed brown sugar
4 eggs
1 teaspoon vanilla extract
1 teaspoon lemon juice
3 cups flour
2 teaspoons baking soda
1 1/2 teaspoons salt
1 teaspoon cinnamon
1/2 cup rolled oats
4 cups semisweet chocolate chips
2 cups chopped walnuts

Combine the butter, shortening, sugar and brown sugar in a mixing bowl. Beat with an electric mixer at high speed for 5 minutes or until light and fluffy. Add the eggs 1 at a time, beating well after each addition. Beat in the vanilla and lemon juice.

Mix the flour, baking soda, salt, cinnamon and oats in a bowl. Add to the butter mixture gradually and beat until mixed. Stir in the chocolate chips and walnuts. Drop by spoonfuls 2 inches apart onto nonstick cookie sheets.

Bake at 325 degrees for 17 minutes for soft cookies or bake at 350 degrees for 18 minutes for crisp cookies. Remove the cookies to a wire rack to cool.

Yield: 4 to 5 dozen

Double-Chocolate Chip Cookies

1 3/4 cups flour
1/4 teaspoon baking soda
1 cup (2 sticks) butter or margarine, softened
1 teaspoon vanilla extract
1 cup sugar
1/2 cup packed dark brown sugar
1 egg
1/3 cup baking cocoa
2 tablespoons milk
1 cup chopped pecans or walnuts
1 cup semisweet chocolate chips

Mix the flour and baking soda in a bowl. Beat the butter in a bowl with an electric mixer until light and fluffy. Beat in the vanilla, sugar and brown sugar. Add the egg and beat well. Beat in the baking cocoa at low speed. Add the milk and beat until mixed. Add the dry ingredients, stirring just until blended. Stir in the pecans and chocolate chips.

Drop by rounded teaspoonfuls 2 inches apart onto nonstick cookie sheets or cookie sheets lined with foil. Bake at 350 degrees for 12 to 13 minutes. Cool on the cookie sheets slightly. Remove to wire racks and cool completely.

Yield: 3 dozen

Grand Prize Winner

The grand prize–winning recipe of all 2,600 submitted to The Orchards' contest in 1987 is this rich, moist, double-chocolate cookie. The cookies were judged by three editors from Chocolatier, Orchards pastry chef Heather Andrus, and Chester and Carol Soling, owners of the inn. Each judge was allowed three minutes to savor each cookie and rank it on a scale of one to ten. Sips of cold milk, water, or Champagne cleared their palates for the next tasting. This recipe has appeared in two editions of The Perfect Chocolate Chip Cookie *and in our first cookbook,* Winning at the Table.

Crispy Chocolate Sticks

1 ounce unsweetened chocolate
1/4 cup (1/2 stick) butter
1 egg
1/2 cup sugar
1/4 cup flour
1/4 cup chopped pecans
2 tablespoons butter, softened
1 cup confectioners' sugar
1 tablespoon heavy cream or evaporated milk
1 ounce unsweetened chocolate
1 tablespoon butter

Melt 1 ounce chocolate and 1/4 cup butter in a small saucepan. Remove from the heat and let cool slightly. Beat the egg in a bowl until foamy. Stir in the sugar and melted chocolate mixture. Add the flour and pecans. Stir until well mixed. Pour the batter into a greased and floured 8×8-inch baking pan. Bake at 350 degrees for 20 minutes. Let cool on a wire rack.

Mix 2 tablespoons butter, the confectioners' sugar and cream in a bowl. Beat until blended. Spread over the cooled cookie layer. Chill for 15 minutes or longer.

Melt 1 ounce chocolate and 1 tablespoon butter in a small saucepan. Stir until blended. Drizzle over the chilled filling layer. Tilt the pan to spread the chocolate glaze evenly. Chill for 1 hour or longer. Cut into 1×2-inch rectangles with a sharp knife. Arrange on a serving plate and chill until ready to serve.

NOTE: If a thicker glaze is desired, increase the chocolate to 1 1/2 ounces and the butter to 1 1/2 tablespoons.

Yield: 32 servings

Pumpkin Bars

4 eggs
1 cup vegetable oil
2 cups sugar
1 (15-ounce) can solid-pack pumpkin
2 cups flour
2 teaspoons baking powder
1 teaspoon baking soda
1/2 teaspoon salt
2 teaspoons cinnamon
1/2 teaspoon ground cloves
1/2 teaspoon ginger
1/2 teaspoon nutmeg
8 ounces cream cheese, softened
6 tablespoons butter or margarine, softened
1 tablespoon milk
1 teaspoon vanilla extract
4 cups confectioners' sugar
Orange food coloring
Chopped walnuts

Mix the eggs, vegetable oil, sugar and pumpkin in a bowl. Sift the flour, baking powder, baking soda, salt, cinnamon, cloves, ginger and nutmeg into a bowl. Add to the pumpkin mixture and stir until well mixed. Pour the batter into a greased 12×18-inch baking pan. Bake at 350 degrees for 25 to 30 minutes or until a wooden pick inserted near the center comes out clean. Cool on a wire rack.

Beat the cream cheese and butter in a mixing bowl with an electric mixer until light and fluffy. Beat in the milk and vanilla. Add the confectioners' sugar and beat until smooth. Stir in orange food coloring until the desired shade is reached. Spread the frosting on the cooled cake. Sprinkle with chopped walnuts. Cut into bars.

Yield: 4 dozen

Chocolate Rum Truffles

9 ounces bittersweet or semisweet chocolate, chopped
8 ounces extra-thick double cream
3 tablespoons unsalted butter
2 to 3 tablespoons each dark rum and crème fraîche
6 ounces white chocolate, chopped
2 tablespoons finely chopped pistachios
6 ounces bittersweet or semisweet chocolate, chopped
6 ounces milk chocolate, chopped

Combine 9 ounces bittersweet chocolate, double cream and butter in a saucepan. Cook over low heat until the chocolate and butter are melted. Remove from the heat and whisk in the rum and crème fraîche. Pour the mixture into a bowl lined with plastic wrap. Allow to cool to room temperature. Cover and chill for a few hours or until firm. Turn the chilled filling onto a work surface. Remove and discard the plastic wrap. Divide the mixture into 40 pieces and shape each one gently into a ball. Dust your hands with baking cocoa if the mixture is too sticky. Place the balls on a parchment-lined baking sheet. Chill for 30 minutes.

Place the white chocolate in a small heatproof bowl. Place over a saucepan of simmering water. Heat until melted, stirring until smooth. Remove from the heat and let cool for 10 minutes. Place a truffle on a skewer and hold over the melted white chocolate. Spoon the chocolate over the truffle until coated. Return the truffle to the baking sheet. Repeat with 12 more truffles. Sprinkle with the chopped pistachios.

Place 6 ounces bittersweet chocolate in a small heatproof bowl. Place over a saucepan of simmering water. Heat until melted, stirring until smooth. Remove from the heat and let cool for 10 minutes. Place a truffle on a skewer and hold over the melted bittersweet chocolate. Spoon the chocolate over the truffle until coated. Return the truffle to the baking sheet. Repeat with 12 more truffles. Place the milk chocolate in a small heatproof bowl. Place over a saucepan of simmering water. Heat until melted, stirring until smooth. Remove from the heat and let cool for 10 minutes. Place a truffle on a skewer and hold over the melted milk chocolate. Spoon the chocolate over the truffle until coated. Place back on the baking sheet. Repeat with the remaining truffles. Chill until set. Remove to a serving platter. Serve with fresh fruit.

Yield: 40 truffles

Almond Toffee

This toffee is pictured on page 160.

1 cup finely chopped almonds
2 cups sugar
2 cups (4 sticks) butter
1/4 cup water
2 tablespoons light corn syrup
2 cups semisweet chocolate chips
3 tablespoons finely chopped almonds

Sprinkle 1 cup chopped almonds in a buttered 9×13-inch baking pan. Combine the sugar, butter, water and corn syrup in a heavy saucepan. Cook over medium heat to 290 degrees on a candy thermometer, soft-crack stage, stirring constantly. Cooking time should be about 20 to 25 minutes.

Pour the candy over the chopped almonds in the pan. Tilt the pan to coat evenly. Sprinkle with the chocolate chips. Let stand for 2 minutes or until the chocolate is melted.

Spread the chocolate evenly over the top of the toffee. Sprinkle with 3 tablespoons chopped almonds. Break into pieces with a knife when cool.

Yield: about 2 pounds

Junior League Contributions to UNLV

Funding for Nevada Southern Building Fund

UNLV Special Collections Library

First UNLV Student Loan Fund

Funding for First Well

Funding for first Student Union

Funding for Museum of Natural Science and Docent Development

UNLV Museum Project (Marjorie Barrick Museum of Natural History)

Established Fussel Education Chair

Established Library Endowment Fund

Funding for library books for UNLV

Funding for Performing Arts Center

Orange Nut Balls

1 (12-ounce) package vanilla wafers, crushed
1 (1-pound) package confectioners' sugar
1 cup chopped pecans
1 (6-ounce) can frozen orange juice concentrate, thawed
1/2 cup (1 stick) butter, softened
1 cup flaked coconut

Mix the vanilla wafers, confectioners' sugar and pecans in a bowl. Add the orange juice concentrate and butter. Stir until well mixed. Shape into bite-size balls. Spread the coconut on a plate. Roll the balls in the coconut. Store in an airtight container and chill until ready to serve.

NOTE: Dip your hands in cold water occasionally when rolling to prevent sticking.

Yield: 4 dozen

Pecan Balls

1 cup (2 sticks) butter, softened
1/2 cup sugar
1/2 teaspoon salt
1 teaspoon vanilla extract
2 cups sifted flour
2 cups finely chopped pecans
Confectioners' sugar

Beat the butter and sugar in a mixing bowl with an electric mixer until fluffy. Stir in the salt and vanilla. Add the flour gradually and stir until mixed. Stir in the pecans. Cover and chill for several hours. Shape into 1-inch balls and place on ungreased baking sheets. Bake at 350 degrees for 12 to 15 minutes. Remove to a wire rack and let cool slightly. Roll in confectioners' sugar while warm.

VARIATION: Substitute almond extract for the vanilla extract and chopped almonds for the chopped pecans.

Yield: 5 dozen

Sugar-and-Spice Pecans

This snack is pictured on page 160.

1 egg
1 tablespoon cold water
1 pound pecan, walnut or almond halves
1/2 cup sugar
1 teaspoon cinnamon
1/4 teaspoon ground cloves
1/4 teaspoon salt

Beat the egg and cold water in a bowl. Stir in the pecans. Mix the sugar, cinnamon, cloves and salt in a bowl. Add to the pecan mixture and stir until mixed.

Spread the pecans in a single layer on a nonstick baking sheet. Bake at 225 degrees for 1 hour, turning the pecans every 15 minutes. Let cool before serving.

Yield: 1 pound

Las Vegas "Suites" Menu

Holiday Slush (page 21)

Fabulous Eggnog (page 77)

Almond Toffee (page 167)

Orange Nut Balls (page 168)

Sugar-and-Spice Pecans (at left)

Chocolate Mousse Pie (page 170)

Pumpkin Swirl Cheesecake (page 180)

Chocolate Mousse Pie

3 cups chocolate wafer crumbs
1 cup (2 sticks) unsalted butter, melted
16 ounces semisweet chocolate, chopped
2 eggs
4 egg yolks
4 egg whites
2 cups whipping cream
6 tablespoons confectioners' sugar
2 cups whipping cream
1 tablespoon sugar

Mix the crumbs with the melted butter in a bowl. Press onto the bottom and up the side of a buttered 10-inch springform pan. Chill for 2 hours or longer. Melt the chocolate in a double boiler. Remove from the heat and pour into a large bowl. Let cool slightly. Beat in 2 eggs quickly. Beat in the 4 egg yolks quickly. Beat the egg whites in a bowl until stiff but not dry. Combine 2 cups whipping cream and the confectioners' sugar in a bowl. Beat until soft peaks form. Beat a small amount of the beaten egg whites and a small amount of the whipped cream into the chocolate mixture. Fold in the remaining egg whites and whipped cream gently.

Pour into the chilled crust. Cover and chill for 6 hours to overnight. Combine 2 cups whipping cream and the sugar in a bowl. Beat until soft peaks form. Spread on top of the filling. Garnish with chocolate curls. Loosen the pie from the side of the pan with a sharp knife and remove the side of the pan.

NOTE: This pie may be frozen for up to 2 weeks before adding the whipped cream and chocolate curls. Cover and wrap well. To avoid raw eggs that may carry salmonella, use an equivalent amount of egg substitute.

Yield: 12 to 16 servings

Rum Cream Pie

4 egg yolks
3/4 cup sugar
1 envelope unflavored gelatin
1/2 cup cold water
2 cups whipping cream
1 teaspoon vanilla extract
2 tablespoons rum
1 (9-inch) graham cracker pie shell
2 squares bittersweet chocolate, shaved

Beat the egg yolks in a mixing bowl until light. Beat in the sugar gradually. Combine the gelatin and cold water in a saucepan. Let stand for 1 minute. Place over low heat and cook until the gelatin is dissolved, stirring constantly. Pour into the egg mixture in a slow stream, beating constantly. Set aside to cool.

Whip the cream in a mixing bowl until stiff peaks form. Stir in the vanilla and rum. Fold the whipped cream into the egg mixture. Spoon into the pie shell, mounding in the center. Sprinkle with the shaved chocolate. Chill until set.

Yield: 8 servings

Fabulous Fudge Pie

1/2 cup (1 stick) butter, melted
1 (16-ounce) package chocolate chips
1 cup sugar
1/2 cup flour
2 eggs
1 teaspoon vanilla extract
1/2 cup chopped walnuts or pecans
1 unbaked (9-inch) pie shell

Mix the butter and chocolate chips in a bowl. Stir in the sugar. Add the flour and mix well. Stir in the eggs. Add the vanilla and mix well. Stir in the walnuts. Pour into the pie shell. Bake at 350 degrees for 45 to 55 minutes or until the top has a light brown crust. Cool completely on a wire rack. Serve with whipped cream.

Yield: 8 servings

Italian Apple Tart

2 apples, peeled, cored, sliced
1 prepared Marsala Tart Pastry (page 173)
2 eggs
1/2 cup sugar
2 tablespoons flour
1 1/4 cups ricotta cheese
1/4 teaspoon salt
2 teaspoons grated lemon peel
1/2 cup light cream
1/4 cup raisins

Arrange the apple slices evenly in the pastry shell. Combine the eggs and sugar in a bowl. Beat with an electric mixer at high speed until thick. Beat in the flour, ricotta cheese, salt, lemon peel and cream at low speed. Fold in the raisins. Pour over the apples. Bake at 350 degrees for 45 minutes to 1 hour or until golden brown. Serve warm or at room temperature.

NOTE: Place foil around the edge of the crust if the crust is browning too quickly during baking.

Yield: 8 servings

Marsala Tart Pastry

1 1/4 cups flour
1/2 teaspoon salt
1/2 teaspoon cinnamon
1/4 cup sugar
1 teaspoon baking powder
2 teaspoons grated lemon peel
1/2 cup (1 stick) butter, cut into 1/2-inch pieces
1 egg yolk
2 tablespoons marsala

Sift the flour, salt, cinnamon, sugar and baking powder into a bowl. Stir in the lemon peel. Add the butter. Mix with your fingers until the mixture has the consistency of coarse cornmeal.

Beat the egg yolk and marsala in a small bowl. Add to the flour mixture. Stir until the dough forms a ball. Place between lightly floured sheets of waxed paper. Roll out to fit a 9-inch pie plate. Fit into the pie plate and place in the freezer for 5 minutes. Bake at 400 degrees for 5 minutes. Cool on a wire rack before filling.

Yield: 1 pie pastry

Death Valley

In 1849, a group of pioneers entered the valley thinking it was a shortcut to California. After barely surviving the journey across the area, the pioneers named it Death Valley. The Death Valley National Monument is located approximately 140 miles and 2 1/2 hours north of Las Vegas. Known for its arid and barren appearance, Death Valley is actually a fascinating, beautiful place to visit. At 280 feet below sea level, it is the lowest elevation in North America. It is filled with historical sites and provides a variety of recreational activities, such as golfing, camping, and hiking.

Apple Crumble Tarts

The recipes on these two pages were provided by chef James Wierzelewski.

1/4 cup cornstarch
1/2 cup apple juice
1/2 cup (1 stick) unsalted butter
3 pounds Granny Smith apples, peeled, cored, chopped
1/2 orange, peeled, seeded, chopped
1/2 lemon, peeled, seeded, chopped
1 1/4 cups packed brown sugar
1 1/2 teaspoons cinnamon
1/4 cup pecan pieces
6 tablespoons golden raisins
Sweet Tart Pastry (page 175)
Brown Sugar Topping (page 175)

Stir the cornstarch and apple juice in a small bowl until the cornstarch is dissolved. Melt the butter in a shallow saucepan. Add the apples, orange and lemon and toss to coat. Stir in the brown sugar, cinnamon, pecans and raisins. Stir in the cornstarch mixture. Cook until the mixture becomes thick and clear. Remove from the heat and let cool.

Roll out the Sweet Tart Pastry on a floured work surface to a thickness of 1/8 inch. Lay the dough in the bottom of a glass baking dish. Pour the apple filling on top and spread evenly over the dough. Sprinkle with the Brown Sugar Topping.

Bake at 350 degrees for 25 minutes or until the topping is golden brown and the filling is bubbly. Cool completely on a wire rack. Cut tarts out with a 2-inch round cookie cutter. Serve with maple ice cream and caramel sauce.

Yield: 20 tarts

Sweet Tart Pastry

3/4 cup plus 2 tablespoons unsalted butter, softened
1/3 cup sugar
1 egg
1 egg yolk
1 teaspoon vanilla extract
1/2 teaspoon salt
2 1/3 cups flour

Combine the butter and sugar in a mixing bowl. Beat with an electric mixer until light and fluffy. Add the egg, egg yolk and vanilla and mix well. Add the salt and flour and mix until a smooth dough forms. Shape into a ball. Cover and chill for 40 minutes or longer before using.

Yield: 1 tart pastry

Brown Sugar Topping

1 1/2 cups (3 sticks) unsalted butter, softened
1 1/4 cups packed brown sugar
1 cup sugar
1 teaspoon cinnamon
1 1/2 teaspoons nutmeg
1 teaspoon vanilla extract
3 1/2 cups (or more) flour

Beat the butter, brown sugar, sugar, cinnamon, nutmeg and vanilla in a bowl. Add the flour and mix just until crumbly. Add more flour if needed for a crumbly texture.

Yield: 7 1/4 cups

James Wierzelewski

Chef James Wierzelewski of the Parian at the Regent at Summerlin is known for his East-meets-West recipes inspired by his many years of award-winning cooking in Malaysia.

Cappuccino Cheesecake

1 packet (1/3 package) graham crackers
2 tablespoons sugar
1/4 cup (1/2 stick) butter, melted
16 ounces cream cheese, softened
1/2 cup sugar
1 envelope instant decaffeinated mocha-flavored cappuccino
2 eggs
1/4 cup milk
1/2 teaspoon vanilla extract

Crush the graham crackers in a food processor. Add 2 tablespoons sugar and the melted butter. Process until well mixed. Press over the bottom and 1 inch up the side of an 8-inch springform pan. Bake at 350 degrees for 5 minutes. Cool on a wire rack.

Combine the cream cheese, 1/2 cup sugar and instant cappuccino in a bowl. Beat with an electric mixer at medium speed until well blended. Add the eggs, milk and vanilla. Beat until well mixed. Pour into the cooled crust.

Bake at 325 degrees for 40 minutes or until the center is set. Cool on a wire rack. Cover and chill for 3 hours to overnight. Loosen the cheesecake from the side of the pan with a sharp knife and remove the side of the pan. Serve chilled.

Yield: 6 servings

Amaretto Cheesecake

1 cup graham cracker crumbs
1/2 cup (1 stick) butter, melted
1/4 cup sugar
1/2 teaspoon cinnamon
24 ounces cream cheese, softened
1 1/2 cups sugar
1/4 teaspoon almond extract
1/4 cup amaretto
4 eggs
1 1/2 cups sour cream
3 tablespoons vanilla extract
1/4 cup sugar

Mix the graham cracker crumbs, melted butter, 1/4 cup sugar and cinnamon in a bowl. Press the mixture over the bottom of a 9-inch springform pan. Chill for 1 hour or longer.

Beat the cream cheese in a bowl with an electric mixer until light and fluffy. Add 1 1/2 cups sugar, the almond extract and amaretto. Beat for 5 to 10 minutes. Add the eggs 1 at a time, beating for 5 minutes after each addition. Pour the batter into the chilled crust. Bake at 350 degrees for 1 hour. Cool on a wire rack for 20 minutes.

Combine the sour cream, vanilla and 1/4 cup sugar in a bowl. Stir until well mixed. Spread on top of the warm cheesecake. Bake at 350 degrees for 10 minutes. Cool to room temperature on a wire rack. Cover and chill for 3 hours to overnight. Loosen the cheesecake from the side of the pan with a sharp knife and remove the side of the pan. Serve chilled.

Yield: 8 servings

Key Lime Cheesecake

1 cup graham cracker crumbs
3 tablespoons sugar
3 tablespoons butter, melted
24 ounces cream cheese, softened
1 cup sugar
3 tablespoons flour
1 tablespoon grated Key lime peel
3 tablespoons Key lime juice
$1/2$ teaspoon vanilla extract
3 eggs
1 egg white
$3/4$ cup sugar
2 tablespoons cornstarch
$1/2$ cup each cold water and Key lime juice
1 egg yolk, lightly beaten

Mix the graham cracker crumbs, 3 tablespoons sugar and melted butter in a bowl. Press the mixture onto the bottom of a 9-inch springform pan. Bake at 350 degrees for 10 minutes. Cool slightly on a wire rack.

Combine the cream cheese, 1 cup sugar, flour, lime peel, 3 tablespoons lime juice and vanilla in a bowl. Beat with an electric mixer at medium speed until blended. Add the eggs and egg white 1 at a time, beating well after each addition. Pour the batter into the crust. Bake at 350 degrees for 40 minutes. Turn off the oven and leave the cheesecake in the oven until the oven cools. Place on a wire rack and loosen the cheesecake from the side of the pan with a sharp knife. Allow to cool completely before removing the side of the pan.

Combine $3/4$ cup sugar and the cornstarch in a saucepan. Stir in the cold water and $1/2$ cup lime juice gradually. Bring to a boil over medium heat, stirring constantly. Boil for 1 minute or until thickened and clear, stirring constantly. Place the egg yolk in a cup and stir in a small amount of the hot mixture. Return the egg yolk mixture to the saucepan and cook for 3 minutes, stirring constantly. Remove from the heat and let cool slightly. Spread over the cheesecake. Chill for at least 2 hours. Garnish with paper-thin slices of Key lime.

Yield: 8 servings

Formal Dinner Menu

Baked Almond and Crab Appetizer (page 28)

Red and Green Holiday Salad (page 52)

Pecan Carrots (page 86)

Gruyère Potato Gratin (page 89)

Salt-Encrusted Beef Tenderloin (page 101)

Amaretto Cheesecake (page 178)

Pumpkin Swirl Cheesecake

2 cups vanilla wafer crumbs
1/4 cup (1/2 stick) margarine, melted
16 ounces cream cheese, softened
1/2 cup sugar
1 teaspoon vanilla extract
3 eggs
1 cup canned pumpkin
1/4 cup sugar
1 teaspoon cinnamon
1/4 teaspoon nutmeg

Mix the vanilla wafer crumbs and melted margarine in a bowl. Press the mixture onto the bottom and up the side of a 9-inch springform pan. Beat the cream cheese, 1/2 cup sugar and vanilla at medium speed in a bowl until blended. Beat in the eggs 1 at a time.

Reserve 1 cup of the cream cheese mixture and set aside. Add the pumpkin, 1/4 cup sugar, cinnamon and nutmeg to the remaining cream cheese mixture and beat well. Pour half the pumpkin batter into the crust. Top with half the cream cheese batter. Repeat the layers. Cut through the batter several times with a knife for a swirled effect. Bake at 350 degrees for 55 minutes. Cool on a wire rack.

Yield: 10 to 12 servings

Miniature Cheesecakes

12 vanilla wafers
16 ounces cream cheese, softened
1/2 cup sugar
1 teaspoon vanilla extract
2 eggs
Fresh fruit

Line 12 muffin cups with paper or foil liners. Place a vanilla wafer in each muffin cup. Beat the cream cheese, sugar and vanilla at medium speed in a mixing bowl until blended. Beat in the eggs. Fill the muffin cups 3/4 full with batter. Bake at 325 degrees for 25 minutes. Cool in the pan. Top each cheesecake with fresh fruit.

Yield: 12 servings

Pistachio Pastries

2 cups chopped pistachios
2 tablespoons sugar
1 teaspoon cinnamon
1 teaspoon orange water or rose water (see Note)
3 tablespoons clarified butter (page 199)
1 pound phyllo dough
Syrian Syrup (page 182)

Combine the pistachios, sugar, cinnamon, orange water and butter in a bowl. Stir to mix well. (See pages 198 and 199 for directions on working with and shaping the phyllo.) Bake the assembled pastries at 350 degrees for 10 minutes or until light golden brown. Remove to a wire rack and let cool slightly. Drizzle with Syrian Syrup and serve warm.

NOTE: Orange water and rose water can be purchased at Mediterranean grocery stores.

Yield: 10 servings

Sweet Cream Pastries

1/2 cup cold milk
1/4 cup cornstarch
2 cups heavy cream
2 tablespoons sugar
1 teaspoon orange water or rose water
1 pound phyllo dough
Syrian Syrup (below)

Combine the milk and cornstarch in a saucepan. Whisk until the cornstarch is dissolved. Add the cream and sugar. Cook over low heat for 8 minutes or until thickened, whisking constantly. Remove from the heat and stir in the orange water. Let cool to room temperature. (See pages 198 and 199 for directions on working with and shaping the phyllo.) Bake the assembled pastries at 350 degrees for 10 minutes or until light golden brown. Remove to a wire rack and let cool slightly. Drizzle with Syrian Syrup and serve warm.

Yield: 10 servings

Syrian Syrup

1 cup water
2 cups sugar
1 teaspoon lemon juice
1 teaspoon orange water or rose water

Combine the water, sugar and lemon juice in a saucepan. Bring to a boil over medium-high heat. Reduce the heat to low and simmer for 20 minutes. Remove from the heat and let cool for 5 minutes. Stir in the orange water. Allow to cool to room temperature. May be chilled if desired.

NOTE: Orange water and rose water can be purchased at Mediterranean grocery stores.

Yield: 1 1/2 cups

Grand Marnier Ice Cream

This recipe was provided by chef Jean-Louis Palladin.

1 1/2 cups heavy cream
1 cup milk
1/2 cup orange juice
1/4 cup chopped orange peel
7 egg yolks
3/4 cup sugar
6 tablespoons Grand Marnier
Sliced strawberries

Combine the cream, milk, orange juice and orange peel in a heavy 3-quart nonreactive saucepan. Bring to a boil. Remove from the heat and let stand for 15 minutes.

Whisk the egg yolks and sugar in a bowl for 2 minutes or until thick and pale yellow. Return the cream mixture to a boil. Remove from the heat and gradually whisk the hot cream into the egg yolks. Return the mixture to the saucepan. Cook over medium heat for 2 to 3 minutes or just until thickened, stirring constantly. Do not boil. Strain the mixture into a bowl through a chinois or a metal sieve lined with cheesecloth. Use a spoon to push the cream mixture through, leaving the peel behind. Stir in the Grand Marnier.

Cover and chill for at least 3 hours or overnight. Pour into an ice cream freezer container. Freeze using manufacturer's directions. Spoon a scoop into a dessert dish. Top with sliced strawberries.

NOTE: A chinois is a conical stainless steel sieve made of extremely fine wire mesh. The mesh is so fine that a spoon or pestle must be used to press the food through it.

Yield: 1 quart

Jean-Louis Palladin

Considered one of the culinary geniuses of the twentieth century, Chef Jean-Louis Palladin boldly meshes classical traditions with contemporary ideas. This gourmet chef of Italian and French heritage was the 1993 recipient of the James Beard Foundation's Chef of the Year Award. Palladin has worked as a saucier at the Hotel de Paris, at the Plaza Athenee, has opened La Tables Des Cordeliers at the Watergate Hotel in Washington, D.C., and is currently at Napa in the Rio Hotel in Las Vegas. He is one of the pioneers of contemporary cuisine.

Green Tea Ice Cream

2 tablespoons powdered green tea
3 tablespoons boiling water
3 eggs
1 cup light corn syrup
1/2 cup sugar
2 1/4 cups milk
1 1/2 cups heavy cream
1 tablespoon vanilla extract
1 1/2 teaspoons lemon juice
Green and yellow food coloring

Dissolve the tea in the boiling water in a small cup. Set aside and let cool to room temperature. Beat the eggs in a large bowl until foamy. Beat in the corn syrup gradually. Add the sugar and beat until thick. Stir in the cooled tea, milk, cream, vanilla and lemon juice. Stir in a few drops of food coloring until desired color is reached.

Pour the mixture into a 9×13-inch pan. Cover and freeze until almost firm. Remove to a chilled bowl. Beat until smooth. Return to the pan and freeze until firm. Scoop into sherbet glasses. Garnish each serving with a thin narrow strip of lemon peel and a sprig of mint.

Yield: 1 1/2 quarts

Neon Lights Delight

This dessert is pictured on page 148.

3 (3-ounce) packages flavored gelatin (3 different flavors)
3 cups boiling water
1$^{1/2}$ cups cold water
1 envelope unflavored gelatin
$^{1/4}$ cup sugar
1 cup boiling water
$^{1/2}$ cup pineapple juice
2 cups graham cracker crumbs
6 tablespoons butter, melted
2 cups whipping cream

Combine 1 package of flavored gelatin with 1 cup of the 3 cups boiling water in a bowl. Stir until dissolved. Add $^{1/2}$ cup of the cold water and stir to mix. Pour into an 8-inch square baking dish. Repeat with the second and third packages of flavored gelatin and pour into separate 8-inch square baking dishes. Cover and chill for 3 hours to overnight.

Combine the unflavored gelatin, sugar and 1 cup boiling water in a bowl. Stir until dissolved. Stir in the pineapple juice. Chill for 15 minutes or until cooled but not beginning to set.

Mix the graham cracker crumbs and melted butter in a bowl. Press the mixture over the bottom of a 9- or 10-inch springform pan.

Whip the cream in a bowl with an electric mixer until stiff. Fold in the pineapple mixture. Cut the flavored gelatin into $^{1/2}$-inch cubes with a knife. Scrape the cubes gently out of the dishes with a rubber spatula and fold into the whipped cream. Spoon the mixture into the crust. Cover and chill for 6 hours to overnight. Loosen the filling from the side of the pan with a sharp knife and remove the side of the pan. Serve chilled.

Yield: 8 to 10 servings

Casa Vega Flan

3/4 cup sugar
4 eggs
1 teaspoon vanilla extract
2 cups sweetened condensed milk
1/4 cup sugar

Caramelize 3/4 cup sugar in a skillet over medium heat, stirring constantly until the sugar is melted and golden brown. Pour into a 4-cup ring mold. Tilt the mold quickly to coat the sides and bottom. Beat the eggs and vanilla in a mixing bowl. Mix the condensed milk and 1/4 cup sugar in a bowl. Whisk the milk mixture into the eggs. Pour over the caramelized sugar in the mold.

Place the mold in a larger baking pan. Add water to the larger pan to a depth of 1 inch. Bake at 350 degrees for 45 minute to 1 hour or until a knife inserted near the center comes out clean. Cool completely on a wire rack. Invert the flan onto a large plate.

Yield: 6 to 8 servings

Mint Julep Parfaits

1/2 gallon French vanilla ice cream
1 cup crème de menthe
1/2 cup bourbon

Soften the ice cream in a bowl. Stir in the crème de menthe and bourbon. Spoon into 8 parfait glasses. Freeze for several hours or until firm.

Yield: 8 servings

Bittersweet Chocolate Bread Pudding

This recipe was provided by Susan Massey.

2 cups milk
4 ounces bittersweet chocolate, chopped
3/4 cup sugar
1/4 cup (1/2 stick) butter
1 cup milk
2 teaspoons vanilla extract
1/2 teaspoon cinnamon
1/4 teaspoon nutmeg
8 ounces buttermilk white bread, cubed (about 5 cups)
3 eggs, beaten

Heat 2 cups milk in a saucepan until just below the boiling point. Remove from the heat. Add the chocolate and stir until melted. Add the sugar and butter and stir until the sugar is dissolved and the butter is melted. Let cool for 10 minutes. Pour into a large bowl. Stir in 1 cup milk, vanilla, cinnamon, nutmeg and bread cubes. Add the eggs and stir gently to mix. Spoon into a buttered 1 1/2-quart baking dish or soufflé dish.

Bake at 350 degrees for 45 minutes or until the center moves slightly when shaken. Let stand on a wire rack for 15 minutes. Serve warm with whipped cream. Garnish with chocolate shavings.

Yield: 6 servings

Susan Massey

Susan Massey has been a professional food stylist in San Francisco for 20 years. Her work includes print advertising, television commercials, and numerous cookbook publications. She has styled books for Chuck Williams and Joyce Goldstein, Williams-Sonoma; Martin Yan, Janet Fletcher, and Letty Flatt of Deer Valley Lodge; Joyce Jue; and Joanne Weir.

Her Las Vegas restaurant clients include Gatsby's, Mark Miller's Coyote Cafe, Emeril LaGasse's New Orleans Fish House, Wolfgang Puck's Cafe, The Brown Derby Restaurant, and Neyla's Moroccan Restaurant.

She now resides in Salt Lake City.

Raisin Bread Pudding

4 to 5 slices raisin bread
Softened butter
1 cup sugar
3 eggs
1/4 cup (1/2 stick) butter, softened
1 (12-ounce) can evaporated milk
1 cup milk
1/2 teaspoon nutmeg
1 tablespoon vanilla extract

Butter the bread with softened butter and place on a baking sheet. Place under the broiler until toasted and golden brown. Remove the toast to a wire rack to cool. Combine the sugar, eggs and 1/4 cup butter in a bowl. Stir with a fork just until mixed. Stir in the evaporated milk, milk, nutmeg and vanilla. Tear the toast into small pieces and add to the milk mixture. Stir until well mixed. Spoon into a greased 9×13-inch baking dish.

Bake at 350 degrees for 45 minutes or until the top is golden brown and the center moves slightly when shaken. Serve warm or at room temperature.

NOTE: You may use white bread and add raisins. Increase the sugar to 1 1/2 cups if using white bread.

Yield: 6 servings

Creamy Rice Pudding

6 cups milk
1 cup uncooked white rice
3/4 cup sugar
1/4 teaspoon salt
2 teaspoons vanilla extract
1 cup whipping cream
1/4 teaspoon nutmeg

Combine the milk, rice, sugar and salt in a 3-quart saucepan. Cook over medium heat until tiny bubbles form around the edge, stirring frequently. Reduce the heat to low and cover. Simmer for 1 hour or until the rice is very tender, stirring occasionally. Stir in the vanilla. Pour into a bowl. Cover and chill for at least 3 hours or overnight.

Whip the cream in a bowl with an electric mixer at medium speed until soft peaks form. Fold the whipped cream into the chilled rice mixture. Spoon into dessert dishes and sprinkle with nutmeg.

VARIATION: Combine 1/2 cup raisins with 1/4 cup bourbon or rum in a bowl. Let soak for 1 hour or longer. Add to the milk and rice mixture before cooking.

Yield: 10 servings

The Meadows, Snow-Topped

Mexican trader Antonio Armijo, leading a 60-man party along the Spanish Trail to Los Angeles in 1829, veered from the accepted route. On Christmas Day, while Armijo's caravan was camped about 100 miles northeast of present-day Las Vegas, a scouting party rode west in search of water. Rafael Rivera, an experienced young Mexican scout, left the party and ventured into the unexplored desert. Within two weeks, he discovered Las Vegas Springs. The abundant artesian spring water discovered at Las Vegas Springs shortened the Spanish Trail to Los Angeles and hastened the rush west for California gold. Between 1830 and 1848, the name "Vegas," as shown on maps of that day, was changed to Las Vegas, which means "the meadows" in Spanish. Nevada is Spanish for "snow-topped."

Tuaca Orange Crème Brûlée

This recipe was provided by chef Stanton Ho (see sidebar, page 157).

9 egg yolks
3 tablespoons Tuaca liqueur
1/2 teaspoon finely grated orange peel
3 cups heavy cream
1 cup milk
1 vanilla bean, scraped
1 teaspoon vanilla extract
3/4 cup plus 2 tablespoons sugar
1/8 teaspoon salt
6 tablespoons superfine sugar

Mix the egg yolks, liqueur and orange peel in a bowl. Combine the cream, milk, vanilla bean, vanilla extract, sugar and salt in a saucepan. Heat to just below the boiling point. Remove from the heat. Whisk half the hot cream mixture slowly into the egg yolk mixture. Add the egg yolk mixture and cream mixture to the saucepan. Return to the heat and cook until hot, stirring constantly. Do not boil. Strain through a sieve into a bowl.

Divide the mixture among nine 4-ounce ovenproof custard cups. Place the cups in a large baking pan. Add water to the pan to a depth of 1 inch. Place a foil tent over the pan. Bake at 325 degrees for 45 minutes. Cool to room temperature on a wire rack. Cover and chill for 2 hours or longer. Sprinkle the top of the custards with the superfine sugar. Caramelize the sugar under a broiler. Serve with fresh berries or other fresh fruit.

Yield: 9 servings

Bananas Foster

This recipe was provided by chef Chris Johns.

1/4 cup (1/2 stick) butter
3/4 cup packed brown sugar
Grated peel and juice of 1 orange
Grated peel and juice of 1 lemon
4 bananas, halved lengthwise
1/4 cup banana liqueur
3 tablespoons rum
2 tablespoons brandy
4 scoops vanilla ice cream

Melt the butter in a skillet over medium heat. Add the brown sugar and cook until the brown sugar is dissolved, stirring constantly. Stir in the orange peel and lemon peel. Simmer for 1 minute. Stir in the orange juice and lemon juice. Cook until reduced by 1/2.

Add the bananas to the brown sugar mixture and cook until heated through. Add the banana liqueur, rum and brandy. Increase the heat to high and heat until hot. Remove from the heat and ignite with a match. Serve over ice cream when the flames subside.

Yield: 4 servings

Chris Johns

Chris Johns is the Executive Chef for the Orleans Hotel. His tasty creations can be sampled at the Canal Street Grill.

Passion Fruit Syllabub

4 passion fruit
Grated peel and juice of 2 limes
2 to 3 tablespoons medium-sweet sherry
1 cup whipping cream
1/4 cup (or more) sugar
1 passion fruit

Cut the 4 passion fruit into halves. Scoop out the seeds and pulp and place in a measuring cup. Add the lime peel and juice. Add enough sherry to measure 2/3 cup.

Combine the cream and sugar in a bowl. Beat with an electric mixer at medium speed until thickened. Reduce the speed to low and add the fruit mixture gradually. Beat just until the cream holds firm peaks. Test for sweetness and add more sugar if desired.

Spoon the syllabub into dessert dishes. Cut 1 passion fruit into halves. Spoon some of the seeds and pulp onto each serving. Garnish with a twist of lime and a mint leaf. Chill until serving time.

Yield: 4 to 6 servings

Desert Pizza

This recipe was provided by Stephanie Markham.

2 bananas, sliced
3 to 4 kiwifruit, peeled, sliced
1 1/2 cups strawberries, hulled, sliced
Juice of 2 lemons
1 (2-layer) package white cake mix
1/2 cup (1 stick) butter, melted
16 ounces cream cheese, softened
1/2 cup sugar
1 teaspoon vanilla extract
1/3 cup sour cream
Melted chocolate (optional)

Arrange the bananas, kiwifruit and strawberries on a plate. Sprinkle with the lemon juice to prevent browning. Place the cake mix in a bowl. Add the melted butter gradually and mix with a fork until crumbly. Spread the mixture on a nonstick 14- to 16-inch pizza pan. Pat the dough into an even layer. Bake at 350 degrees for 20 to 30 minutes or until lightly browned, checking the dough every 10 minutes while baking. If starting to rise, press the dough down gently with a towel. Cool completely on a wire rack.

Combine the cream cheese, sugar, vanilla and sour cream in a bowl. Beat with an electric mixer until smooth and creamy. Spread the cream cheese mixture evenly over the pizza crust, leaving 1/2-inch edge of crust exposed. Layer the fruit over the top. Drizzle with melted chocolate. Cover and chill for 3 hours or longer. Slice and serve cold.

NOTE: Both the crust and cream cheese filling can be made up to 1 day ahead. Cover the crust and store at room temperature. Cover the cream cheese filling and store in the refrigerator.

Yield: 10 to 12 servings

Stephanie Markham

Stephanie Markham has been the food editor of Nevada Woman *magazine since its inception in 1995. Her love of entertaining comes from living for several years in the south of France, where, she says, "Everyone throws dinner parties." Her favorite cuisine is Italian and "anything my husband prepares," says Stephanie.*

She believes that entertaining should be effortless–simple preparation with fabulous presentation. Stephanie resides in Las Vegas with her husband Clay, daughter Madison, and two kitty cats.

Grilled Fruit

1/4 cup (1/2 stick) butter, melted
1/4 cup packed dark brown sugar
1 teaspoon cinnamon
4 yellow or white peaches, halved
4 red plums, halved
4 bananas, quartered

Mix the butter, brown sugar and cinnamon in a bowl. Add the peaches, plums and bananas and toss to coat. Arrange the fruit cut side down on a foil-lined broiler pan. Broil for 10 minutes or until caramelized and browned. Turn the fruit over and broil for 10 minutes longer. Rearrange the fruit as needed to prevent burning. Serve warm with ice cream.

NOTE: The fruit can be grilled instead of broiled.

Yield: 4 servings

Frozen Fruit Cups

2 cups sour cream
1 (8-ounce) can crushed pineapple
3/4 cup sugar
2 tablespoons lemon juice
1/4 cup chopped pecans
3 bananas, sliced
1 cup sliced strawberries

Line 12 muffin cups with paper or foil liners. Mix the sour cream, pineapple, sugar, lemon juice, pecans, bananas and strawberries in a bowl. Spoon the mixture into the muffin cups. Freeze until firm. Serve frozen.

NOTE: Once frozen, the fruit cups can be removed from the muffin tin and stored in a freezer bag.

Yield: 12 servings

Very Berry Crisp

This recipe was provided by Susan Anton.

1 cup flour
1 cup sugar
1 teaspoon baking powder
1/2 teaspoon salt
1 or 2 eggs, beaten
5 to 6 cups berries, such as raspberries, strawberries,
   blueberries, blackberries, or a combination
2 tablespoons flour
1/2 cup (or more) sugar
1/2 cup (1 stick) butter, melted

Mix 1 cup flour, 1 cup sugar, baking powder and salt in a bowl.
Make a well in the center and add 1 beaten egg in the well.
Stir with a fork until the mixture resembles coarse cornmeal.
Add more beaten egg if the mixture is too dry.

Place the berries in a large bowl. Mix 2 tablespoons flour and
1/2 cup sugar in a bowl. Add more sugar if the berries are tart.
Add to the berries and toss to coat.

Spoon the coated berries evenly into a buttered 8×8-inch
baking dish. Sprinkle the flour mixture evenly over the berries.
Drizzle evenly with the melted butter. Bake at 375 degrees for
40 minutes or until the top is golden brown. Serve warm or
at room temperature with whipped cream or ice cream.

Yield: 6 servings

Susan Anton

*Susan Anton, a former
Miss California, got her
start in Las Vegas at an
early age. She has been
the Muriel cigar girl, has
appeared in* Cliffhangers
and Goldengirl, *and has
recorded a hit country
song. Anton is a regular
performer on the Las Vegas
Strip and is an avid golfer
at TPC Summerlin. She
and her husband have their
own production company.*

Melon in Rum Lime Sauce

This dessert is pictured on page 68.

1 cantaloupe
1 small honeydew melon
1/8 of a small watermelon
1 cup fresh blueberries
2/3 cup sugar
1/3 cup water
1 teaspoon grated lime peel
6 tablespoons fresh lime juice
1/2 cup light rum (optional)

Shape all the melons into balls using a melon ball scoop. Place in a bowl and add the blueberries. Cover and chill. Mix the sugar and water in a small saucepan. Bring to a boil. Reduce the heat and simmer for 4 minutes. Stir in the lime peel, lime juice and rum. Remove from the heat and let cool slightly.

Pour the rum mixture over the chilled fruit and stir gently to mix. Cover and chill for several hours. Spoon into sherbet glasses and garnish with mint sprigs. Add a splash of rum.

NOTE: This makes a refreshing light dessert or first course.

Yield: 10 to 12 servings

Hot Apple Pie

2 quarts apple juice
3/4 cup cranberry juice
2 cinnamon sticks
1 teaspoon ground cinnamon
1/2 teaspoon whole cloves
1/4 cup sugar
Tuaca liqueur to taste
Whipped cream

Combine the apple juice, cranberry juice, cinnamon sticks, ground cinnamon, cloves and sugar in a large saucepan and stir to mix. Simmer for several hours or until the spices fall to the bottom of the pan.

Strain into cups and add the liqueur to taste. Top with whipped cream.

Yield: 6 to 8 servings

Working with Phyllo

Helpful Hints

Phyllo is available frozen at supermarkets (and sometimes fresh in Greek and Middle Eastern markets). Thaw it, unopened, overnight in the refrigerator.

Unroll the thawed but still chilled dough onto a sheet of waxed paper. Keep the unused portion of the dough covered with waxed paper topped with a damp towel to prevent it from drying out while you are working. Refrigerate or refreeze any dough that you do not need.

Use ungreased baking sheets with sides.

Have handy a sharp knife or pizza cutter, kitchen scissors, a wide pastry brush, and a spoon.

Work quickly while the dough remains moist and flexible. Directions for buttering and shaping the dough are given below.

After assembly, you may refrigerate the phyllo, covered with plastic wrap, for up to 24 hours. Then bake according to the recipe directions. You may also freeze filled phyllo; simply thaw before baking.

A golden to golden brown crust is the goal. If browning occurs too quickly, simply cover with a sheet of foil.

Syrups and fillings in this book can be prepared one to two days ahead of the assembling of the filled phyllo. Store fillings in the refrigerator until needed.

Shaping and Cooking Phyllo

The versatility of phyllo is evidenced by the many shapes and sizes that can be created. For triangles, rolls, and squares, work with one sheet of phyllo at a time. Place the sheet in front of you with the short ends on your left and right. Brush the sheet lightly with melted clarified butter (see Clarified Butter, at right). Fold the sheet in half like a book and again brush lightly with clarified butter. Cut the dough into the desired shapes using the directions that follow here. Place the correct amount of filling on the dough, wrap, and place seam side down on the baking sheet. When all the filling has been used, brush each pastry lightly with clarified butter. Bake at 350 degrees for 10 minutes or until golden brown.

Triangles

For appetizers, cut the dough into four equal strips. Place 1 tablespoon of the filling at the bottom of each strip.

For entrées, cut the dough into two equal strips. Place 2 tablespoons of the filling at the bottom of the strips.

Fold flag-style by taking the lower left-hand corner of the dough and folding it diagonally over the filling to the right edge of the dough strip. Do this working back and forth to the end of the dough strip. You will have a finished triangle.

Rolls

For appetizers, cut the dough into 4 equal rectangles. Place 1 tablespoon of the filling down the lower center portion of the rectangle.

For entrées, cut the dough into halves. Place 2 tablespoons of the filling down the lower center portion of the rectangle.

Fold the sides of the dough to meet in the center. Roll up into the shape of a cigar.

Squares

Cut the dough into the same dimensions as for rolls.

Place the filling at the bottom center.

Fold the sides of the dough to meet in the center. Fold in half to make a square.

Clarified Butter

Cut 1 pound of unsalted butter into small pieces. Melt the butter in a saucepan over medium heat. After the butter has melted, simmer gently for 10 to 15 minutes. Skim off any foam from the top. Then pour off the clear (clarified) butter, leaving behind the milky residue. The clarified butter can be stored in the refrigerator for up to one month.

Contributors and Testers

Helen Aberle
Caroline Adams
Diane Adams
Jennifer Adams
Joni Akselrad
Evelyn Allawas
Sylvia Allawas
Janice Allen
Kate Allen
Suzie Alphin
Ann Alsup
Bill Alsup
Donna Andress
Madeleine Andress
Hope Anstett
Julie Anthony
Shannon Anwar
Kathy Augustine
Jeanette Barrett
Mick Batoni
Judy Beal
Sherry Beatty
Sally Bedotto
Barbare Bellino
Judi Bellino
Butch Benda
Michelle Benda
Erin Bendavid
Susan Bernhardt
Lisa Bigleman
Laura Birmingham
Carolyn Bishop
Linda Bixler
Janet Bjerke
Larry E. Black
Sharna Blumenfeld
Susan Borns
Peggy Bostian

Dr. Jane Boudreau
Gretchen Brahier Papez
Sherry Braithwaite
William Braithwaite
Pat Brame
Lucia Bridenstine
Shelly Brink
Patsy Brinton
Kathryn Brock
Monterey Brookman
Susan Brooks
Michele Bruce
Lidia Cambeiro
Susan Campbell
Heidi Canarelli
Becky Cardona
Linda Carter
Mary Cashman
Barbara Cegavske
Bebe Chapman
Bev Chatelain
Michelle Chatigny
Bruce Choueiri
Heather Choueiri-Orfaly
Rhonda Clapp
Donna Cline
Tonya Clutts
Karen Colen
Tricia Conklin
Deni Conrad
Cory Cook
Diana Corazzi
Estelle Cordaseo
Wendy Craft
Carolyn L. Creekmore
Kellie Creekmore-Guild
Jackie Croteau
Marie Crouch

Darlene Curran
Leann Curtis
Kathy Dalvey-Bonar
Linda Darling
Jeanette Davidson
Betty Davis
Debbie Davis
Lynn Dean
Garry De Lucia
Stacy DeMarco
Loretta DeMars
Lydia Denise
Karen Denys
Jeannette DeRoza
Liz Diller
Louise Dillians
Chris Dixon
Mary Gwen
    Dombrowski
Pam Dowell
Anna Downs
Jodell Downs
Mary Downs
Nancy Downs
Nora Downs
Patricia Downs
Christi Doyle
Marna Dreier
Patricia Dunn
Robin Dutchyshyn
Catherine Dwyer
Julia A. Eglet
Kathleen Ellison
Rhonda Evans
Tina Evans
Kathie Faccinto
Denise Facinoli
Toni Fain

Linda Fallon
Anna Farewell
Toni Farn
Kelly Faulkner
Andrea Fee
Barbara Fee
Dave Fee
Jennifer Fee
Terry Felix
Shirley Fentz
Lisa Ferguson
Stephanie Fitzgerald
Marie Nicole Flabi
Dorothy Flauck
Cynthia Follis
Helene Follmer
Lynn Forsythe
Elaine Frazier
Gregg Fusto
Jackie Gallo
Eileen Garber
Nancy L. Gasho
Nancy M. Gasho
Shelly Geiss
Jane Gibbons
John Gibson
Marianne Gibson
Sarah Gielhaug
Kathryn Gillet
Lorraine M. Gingras-
    Gochnour
Dorothy Glim
Gail Goceljak
Joanne Goldberg
Kathy Gommel
Shelley Gorman
Mary Granoski
Patsy Gray

Joanne Greenbaum
Vicki Griffin
Dinah Groce
David Guild
Doug Guild
Grayson Guild
Nanette Guild
Richard Guild
Tashina Guild
Tate Guild
Kris Hadzicki
Maria Hafen
Marti Hafen
Sandy Halseth
Vada Hanlon
Merle Hansen
Sandy Hardesty
Sybille Harges
Michele Hargrave
DM Hattan, Jr.
Beth Hatton
Mary Hayes
Nancy Heberlee
Dale Heidel
Lois Heidel
Sarah Heier
Louise Helton
Allie Hennessy
Barbara Henry
Brian Herman
Debbie Herman
Jessica Herman
Melissa Herman
Paul Herman
Filomena ReDavid
   Holland
Anne Hooser
Ellen Hordan

Betsy Horne
Natalia Hristova
Irene Huff
Dorothy Huffey
Lynne Hunter
Karla Jacobson
Stephanie Jergens
Cheryl Johnson
Eric Johnson
Ken Johnson
Selinda Johnson
Susan Holland Johnson
Wyatt Johnson
Evelyn Johnston
Karen Johnston
Patty Joyce
Wendy Kalb
Julie Keen
Lisa Keener
Carol Kehl
Paul Keith
JoAnn Kelly
John Kelly
Mary Khamsari
Marlene Kirch
Alice Kirschner
Fred Kirschner
D. Annette Kirson
Helen Klatt
Richard Klatt
Wendy Kraft
Jo Ann Krause
Tracey Krause
Amy Kremenek
Katherine Krucker
Julie Krueger
Chuck Kubat
Susan Kubat

LuAnn Kutch
Dick Kwapil
Tanya Laingen
Tricia LaMancusa
Sherry Lane
Gisela Larsen
Trey Layton
Barbara Legarske
Nancy Lenoco
Donald J. Leonard
Lucyann Leonard
Mike Leonard
Nadine Leone
Nancy Leslie
Debbie Levy
Donna Levy
Jenny Levy
Sarah Levy
Carole Lewis
Garlyn Lilly
Mary Lott
June Love
Daunn Loveday
Amy Lucas-Griffin
Patricia Luetkehans
Michel Lujan
Nell Lynn
Mary Macioce
Mardie Macomber
Julie Madden
Andra Maffey
Kathy Mahon, MD
Jennifer Mallinger-Young
Melinda Margolis
Julie Martin
Flora Mason
Kristy Mayor
Sarah McBride

Robbie McClain
Lois McClanathan
Joanne McCormack
Cristen McCormick
Sherry McElmurry
Melinda McGeorge
Paulette McGinley
Rosie McGowan
Denise McGuinn
Anne McGuire
Margaret McKeen
J.J. Medlock
Lisa Melborne
Cynthia Membrila
Shenandoah Merrick
Stefay Miley
Gayle Miller
Sibyl Minden
Theresa Minden
Madelyn Montgomery
Allie Morrow-Roper
Becky Najafi
Betsy Najafi
Dedee Nave
Ulis Newton
Rae Nimmo
Andrew Nixon
Patti Nixon
Joyce Noorda
Bobbi Norris
Pam Nowell
Joan Oberlin
Starr O'Brien
Ron Ogilvie
Kathy Oiness
Bernadette Olden
Denise Olsen
Karen Olsen

Contributors and Testers (continued)

Renee O'Reilly
Alex Orfaly
Robert Orfaly
Marlene Osborn
Patrice Palmer
Angie Palmo
Denise Paskvan
Paula Paul
Debbie Pearsall
Gloria Pearson
Gail M. Peloza
Ann Perlata
Debbie Perlman
Joy Perlman
Janet Perry
Michelle Perry
Leslie Pfaff
Julie Phaneuf
Ruth Pierotti
Carmella Pinto
Karen Poretsky
John Potter
Cindy Pridgen
Ed Prud'homme
Pennye Prud'homme
Linda Prujan
Gail Qualey
Robert Qualey
Janet Raby
Bobbi Randerson
Trudy Rea
Deanna Remark
Jacklyn Rhinehart
Betsy Rhodes
Saundra Richardson
Lisa Riggleman
Penny Robertson
Beth Robinson

Mary Robinson
Stephanie Robinson
Roberta Rohde
Kim Rolston
Jerry Romero
Elizabeth Roper
Nathan Roper
Denise Rose
Joyce Rose-Thompson
Dianne Rousseau
Liz Ruybalid
Sally Rycroft
Ron Sage
Priscilla Scalley
Erin Scalley LeBlanc
Mary Scheer
William Scheer
Katsumi Schlageter
Rita Schlageter
Linda Schmitt
Sharon Schmitt
Summer Schock
Thomas Schock
Julie Schrock
Carolyn Schumacher
Wendy Sebek
Wesley See
Sandy Seiler
Christen Seiter
Michele Shafe
Bruce Shapiro
Carole Shapiro
David Shapiro
Dana Sheehan
Betsy Sheldon
Patricia Shields
Kara Shippee
Judy Sifranii

Angela Simmons
Alcide Simon
Nicole Singleton
Sheryl Slakey
Ann Small
Ed Small
Cathy Snow
Wendy Sobek
Caroline Sobota
Arlene Southard
Myuki Spaar
Maxine Spencer
Toby Spiegal
Stephanie Stallworth
Louise Stepman-Billians
April Stewart
Kit Streit
Carolyn Strong-
    Blumenfeld
Jo Ella Summers
Joan Sunstrum
Kristina Swallow
Judy Sylvain
Noreen Szews
Jane Ray Taylor
Karin Taylor
Margaret Terzich
Juanita Thompson
Janice Titus
Bobby Tone
Joan Tracht
Ann Trobough
Anne Trueblood
Denyce Tuller
Pat McDonnell Twair
Suzanne VanAken
Jacqueline Vaughan
Charleen Vega

Susan Vibe
Chuck Vitale
Peggy Wallander
Jane Walter
Lisa Welborne
Ann Werry
Desiree Whalen
Sandy Wheeler
Christina Wiederholt
Diana Williams
Frankie Williams
Dennis Wirgate
Lynda Wohletz
Julie Wolf
Christine Youtsey
Karen Zamboni
Dedde Zane
Lois Zellers
Megan Zimmer
Janet Zimmerman
Paula Zona

Index

Index

Index

Index

For additional copies of

LAS VEGAS

Glitter to Gourmet

send:
$24.95 plus $4.50 postage and handling for each book
to:
Junior League of Las Vegas
Las Vegas Glitter to Gourmet Cookbook
6170 West Lake Mead Boulevard
PMB 128
Las Vegas, Nevada 89108
or:
Call 702-822-6536 or fax 702-822-6538.

MasterCard or VISA accepted.
Make checks or money orders payable to Junior League of Las Vegas.